# THE PROBLEM WITH
# COGNITIVE BEHAVIOURAL THERAPY

Other titles in the
THE PROBLEM WITH.... Series

*The Problem with Humanistic Therapies*

*The Problem with Psychoanalytic Psychotherapy*

# THE PROBLEM WITH COGNITIVE BEHAVIOURAL THERAPY

*Kirsty Hall and Furhan Iqbal*

## KARNAC

First published in 2010 by
Karnac Books Ltd
118 Finchley Road
London NW3 5HT

British Library Cataloguing in Publication Data

A C.I.P. for this book is available from the British Library

ISBN-13: 978-1-85575-840-7

Typeset by Vikatan Publishing Solutions (P) Ltd., Chennai, India


www.karnacbooks.com

# CONTENTS

There is a famous Chinese curse which runs, "May you live in interesting times". These are interesting times indeed for those who are involved in the enormous task of alleviating emotional distress. If 1 in 4 people are diagnosed at some point in their lives with a recognised form of mental illness and yet there is no magic bullet to cure this vast reservoir of human suffering, then indeed we are living in interesting times.

The threats to human life from external factors such as continuing arenas of war, global warming and feeding the world's vast population also loom. Some of these pressures precipitate illness too. Doctors and nurses working in traditional settings in mental hospitals have been augmented by a wide range of people who possess specialist knowledge in assisting people in distress. The titles of the jobs are familiar to many of us—Psychologists (of many varieties), Psychiatrists, Psychotherapists (also of many varieties), Psychoanalysts, and Counsellors and so on. The list seems endless. To a large extent all are agreed that societies in many countries have a huge problem.

When it comes to solutions, however, few professionals in the field can agree. The pressure exerted by living in interesting times means that the hunt is on to find effective cures for mental illness. The aim of *The Problem with ...* series is to set out the stall for different kinds of therapies and treatments, and then demonstrate that, whatever the proposed solutions, they are not in fact a cure-all; they are accompanied by a series of potentially intractable problems.

In the short space of this preface, at least two problematic assumptions have already been made. A quick visit to the Wikipedia website informs us that the Chinese curse may, in fact, be an urban myth. A more serious question is posed by the words "mentally ill". The term itself presupposes that there is an equal and opposite condition of "mental health". Yet these terms are used to mean very different states of mind in different cultures and at other periods of time than the present.

However, the quasi-mythical Chinese curse has two faces. The experience of interesting times may be difficult—but they are indeed "interesting"! We hope that readers will be interested in these manifold problems. This is a multi-faceted, fascinating field where even the simplest definition can become mired in controversy.

The greatest problem of all that we face is the simple fact of being human. Unadulterated happiness exists only in our dreams—and often eludes us there too. In the meantime, we hope you enjoy reading this series.

Kirsty Hall
Series Editor

# *ACKNOWLEDGEMENTS*

*Kirsty Hall* would like to thank Oliver Rathbone, the Managing Director of Karnac Books. A big thank you to all those who have put up with my unsociable habits over the last few months, particularly Chris who has not seen much of me recently!

*Furhan Iqbal* would like to thank Kirsty Hall for her gentle encouragement throughout the writing of this book. My thanks to Susanne for tolerating my frequent and prolonged withdrawals and especially to Ahmad Shareef who, whilst on holiday, would rather have had me in the pool playing with him than sitting outside writing this book.

# INTRODUCTION

> The good news is that we now have evidence-based
> psychological therapies that can lift at least a half of those
> affected out of their depression or their chronic fear. These
> new therapies are not endless nor backwardlooking treat-
> ments. They are short, forward-looking treatments that
> enable people to challenge their negative thinking and
> build on the positive side of their personalities and situa-
> tions. The most developed of these therapies is cognitive
> behaviour therapy (CBT). (Layard, 2006, p. 4)

The Layard Report catapaulted Cognitive Behavioural Therapy
(CBT) into the forefront of the public imagination. CBT is now a
widely accepted and confidently endorsed psychological intervention practised by a growing number of clinicians. This book
set out to question whether Layard's assertions are entirely jus-
tified. Is CBT the most developed of the therapies? Is a brief
forward-looking treatment always desirable? Does negative
thinking indeed possess the occasional virtue?

In this short book we are not setting out to turn CBT into
a villain. However, any treatment which has hitherto been
greeted with largely uncritical enthusiasm by the press, the

psychiatric and the psychology professions deserves close examination. Like many other treatments for both serious mental illness and mild depression, it has clear advantages and a certain degree of novelty. Not unexpectedly, CBT has also attracted a number of critics. We think that the time has come to offer CBT researchers and practitioners as well as the general public the benefit of a broader subjection to scrutiny of CBT's benefits and limitations.

Although it was originally developed as a method of treating depression, nowadays CBT is used to treat anxiety, panic, phobias, eating disorders, obsessive compulsive disorder, post traumatic stress disorder and even symptoms of schizophrenia. In the media, the assumption is made that it is the treatment of choice for anything from serious mental illness to misery and unhappiness resulting from adversity in life such as being made redundant from your job.

CBT is a therapy that uses cognitive and behavioural techniques to modify cognitions (perceptions, memories, thoughts etc.) to help patients feel better. It aims to produce good results as fast as possible. The therapy concentrates therefore on helping patients set treatment goals and then provides support and encouragement in order to enable patients to achieve these goals through the use of specific cognitive and behavioural techniques. CBT is based on the assumption that our cognitions (perceptions, thoughts etc.) determine both how we feel and how we behave. Information processing lies at the heart of the cognitive model of psychopathology employed in CBT. This assumes that individuals are constantly perceiving, recalling, interpreting and processing information both from the environment and from within. These processes in turn elicit a person's cognitive, emotional and behavioural response to specific events. The responses to such events may be regarded as adaptive or maladaptive in specific situations. The model also posits that biases, distortions, defects in perception and interpretation may lead to maladaptive responses which, if persistent, play an important role in psychopathology (Pretzer and Beck, 1996). The underpinning principle is that a wide range of unpleasant mood states for example, prolonged feelings of depression, anxiety, panic attacks, compulsions, phobia and the like and behaviours such as being withdrawn from society are caused by our faulty ways of thinking about ourselves, our lives and those around us. The prime aim of CBT is therefore to change these faulty ways of thinking.

CBT uses a pragmatic approach to treatment. Its proponents are not primarily interested in philosophical questions about the meaning of illness. They seek fast practical methods of achieving results. The practical approach of CBT is in part also driven by financial imperatives, attempting to bring about adaptive changes in the client, usually using a time limited frame of treatment. Independent of their underpinning theories and claims to efficacy, there is an interesting fundamental problem facing all treatments offered to sufferers from mental illness and CBT is no exception to this. If a government is faced with real choices to be made, such as waging a war, nationalising a failing bank (and supporting many failing banks!) or increased provision of treatments for mental health, the likelihood of the latter receiving funds is small. Mental health is one of the least glamorous areas of medicine and not necessarily high on the public agenda when competing with the more glamorous arenas of cancer treatments and treatments for heart diseases. Much of the research and debate in the field is therefore influenced by saving money and/or maximising profits. In theory, in a democracy, it follows that issues regarding what treatment is appropriate and for whom should be discussed in an open manner. Currently there is a problem in the UK and many other countries. Debate about research is conducted with a view about whether or not the research will result in profit for the organisations concerned. In particular, drugs produce profits for the pharmaceutical industry. Computerised versions of CBT produce profits for software companies. CBT has the capacity to maximise profits for insurance companies as well as health care providers because it is much cheaper to administer than longer-term therapies. The pharmaceutical industry has long been criticised for being market- and profit-driven; however, psychotherapies such as CBT (along with many others) are no exception to this criticism. Training courses for CBT, workshops by the leading lights in the field, publications of books (recommended reading for courses) as well as published rating scales are all, like drugs, a source of financial remuneration for those prepared to tread this path.

There is no space in this free-market model for a discussion about optimal treatments where money is not the prime consideration. Since CBT occupies a dominant position in the market, patients themselves have little or no power to influence any debates that take place. Mental illness and even simple unhappiness are viewed as consumer demands which can be satisfied by providing a range of products. In an ideal world, the value of an individual human life would be held in higher regard. An invidious choice remains; engage in a spurious debate within a spurious frame or subvert the system. The former course flirts with irrelevance. The latter course courts indifference at best or being branded as "unfit to practice" at worst. For these most general of reasons, it is necessary to open a debate about the advantages and disadvantages of CBT. However, in considering the disadvantages of CBT, and there are some of course, we should be careful to avoid apportioning blame when at least some of the causes of its defects should be laid at the door of penny-pinching governments. This book aims to locate CBT in the spectrum of interventions aimed at the relief of emotional suffering. We conclude by assigning it a useful role, where it is not expected to be all things to all people, but rather one tool in a field where it would be desirable to have many options for treatment. Even this view may be an unduly optimistic statement. It has been suggested that those who suffer from depression should be informed that their condition is probably chronic. As the author of a recent paper about treatment of depression commented, "We have begun to be more honest with people about their prognosis. This takes time, but we have had no complaints and compliance has improved. 'This is the first time I have understood the importance of treatment' is the usual response we get from patients. People have a right to the truth." (Andrews, 2001, p. 420) For these reasons, the present authors consider that it might actually benefit those who rely on CBT to know the bad news—that it is not, in fact, a panacea for all ills, simply one choice of treatment amongst many, each of which has limitations and none of which promises a permanent, universal, trouble-free cure.

It is worth noting that, although CBT originated in the United States, both the authors of the book live and work in the UK. Whereas the authors have drawn on international sources, many examples of current practice are based on the British experience. Many of the issues, however, apply to any society where CBT is practised. Chapter One sets out the historical and socio-political background that led to growth of CBT from small beginnings to become the treatment of choice for many ailments. In chapter two, we set out the main constituents of CBT. What do CBT therapists do? How do they think it works? What does the patient do? Chapter three comments on the scientific claims made for CBT. It examines some classic papers which set out the evidence base for CBT and we ask whether this evidence is sufficient to justify the claims made for CBT. We also take a step back and consider whether CBT needs to engage in the philosophical (but also practical) discussions about the very nature of mental illness. Are people who receive CBT always ill? The final chapter assesses the current position of CBT and the advantages it offers as a treatment for a range of ailments and emotional distress.

## CHAPTER ONE

# The historical and socio-political context

The current day phenomenon of what we now know as Cognitive Behavioural Therapy (CBT), probably one of the most widely accepted treatments for a range of psychiatric disorders and psychological problems, is a result of an evolutionary process over a number of decades. During this time, various ideas, theories and influences resulted in the development of the underpinning theory and the clinical practice of CBT. In order to understand the current popularity of CBT, we set out below a short history of its development together with a brief account of the socio-political context which has provided a significant contribution to its success. CBT has its origins in a complex series of rejections, adoptions and adaptations of both psychoanalysis and behaviourism. We will therefore very briefly sketch out the principal features of both these developments.

In the nineteenth century with the process of industrialisation, western societies in particular witnessed change on a scale never seen before. This resulted in a shift from the feudal-agrarian societies, where religion and social hierarchies were established as they had been for many centuries, and although brutal, they provided certainty. In a feudal society everyone knew their place. The advent of industrialised societies, with their emphasis on rationality and a renunciation of religion, led to the abandonment of most of life's certainties. Such changes also challenged the dominant hierarchies of society. Capitalism now came to dominate, although it was in this very context that a Marxist account critical of the very structures of society, with the ruling class and social rules, serving their own class interests also emerged.

The earliest wide-ranging theorisation of a cure for mental illness involving talking as the main form of treatment is to be found in the extensive work of the father of psychoanalysis, Sigmund Freud. In many countries in central Europe, doctors and psychiatrists considered it more important to theorise their work by treating the patient as an object for study in the laboratory. At the end of the nineteenth century it was possible to train as a doctor in Germany or Austria and hardly ever see a patient. As Makari comments, "As professors eagerly focused on their lab work, Vienna's hospitals fell into disrepair" (Makari, 2008, p. 132). By contrast, French psychiatrists at the end of the nineteenth century were much more influenced by what they found in the clinic. For example, Charcot, whose early influence on Freud is well-known, spent much of his time seeing patients in the famous Salpêtrière Hospital in Paris. In his early work, Freud departed from the tradition of speculation tempered by rigorous analytical thinking in two respects. Firstly he used the case study as a means of theorising the causes of emotional distress and implementing a treatment; secondly, he had a habit of incessantly speculating about both sides of a question without necessarily coming down firmly on one side of the fence or another. Both of these attributes, typical of Freud and to some degree of his followers, were quite distinct in character from the approach taken by Americans after Freud's death and after the Second World War.

When the war ended, the world found itself divided into two camps, the capitalist-imperialist camp of western countries and the communist block in the East. It is significant that CBT originated in a post-war world in the West where a triumphant capitalism prevailed. However, the 1950s and 60s also witnessed changes in the loss of traditional dominance on the world stage. The establishment, with its roots in pre-war hierarchies, was under attack.

Psychoanalysis as practised in the USA was dominated by the medical profession for reasons connected with the traditional role of medicine. It was theoretically highly influenced by the work of Freud and his followers. Many of the early analysts who worked and sometimes trained in the United States had known Freud personally.

In its original form, psychoanalysis was derived from Freud's theory that access could be gained to the painful unconscious causes of human emotional suffering through close attention to the words of the patient—the original "talking cure". One of the many results of the transplantation of psychoanalysis in America was a subtle but nevertheless profound change to Freud's theory. Psychoanalysis became a method for listening to the patient but interpretations or other interventions that aimed at changing the way the patient saw his world became passive. The patient had to wait for insight to arrive. Consequently, psychoanalysis often took years with not necessarily much to show for the time and expenditure involved.

Rappaport and his colleagues, Hartmann, Kris and Loewenstein, collectively known as the "ego psychologists", produced an extensive formalisation of Freud's work, which ultimately differed markedly from the original. Patients had to fit the model. No longer did theory adapt to patients. So far as the ego psychologists were concerned, there was a portion of the ego which responded to rational thought. The rational ego could therefore set up what was termed a "working alliance" with the psychoanalyst. As a result, analyst and patient together could work towards adapting the patient's view of the world to the "rational views" of the dominant culture, i.e., that of

20th century capitalism in America. The American consumerist lifestyle was assumed to be equally desirable for all, provided of course the patient (or their insurance company) could afford this. Psychoanalysis, American-style, slowly became out of date. It had become an interminable and prohibitively expensive form of treatment.

Many CBT practitioners in the UK are clinical psychologists or other professionals; they tend to be unaware of CBT's origins as a reaction to the practice of ego psychology in America. Psychoanalysts there became impatient with its ever more rigidified concepts. By the 1960s it took years of expensive training, since American psychoanalysts had to qualify both as medical doctors and as psychoanalysts before setting up in practice and making what (provided one toed the increasingly conservative party line) was a very good living. According to Nathan Hale, "By the late 1960s psychoanalysts averaged an income of $37,000 while psychiatrists were earning $28,000, clinical psychologists $17,000 and psychiatric social workers $11,000 (Hale, 1995, p. 248). The exclusivity of psychoanalysis in terms of both the personalities involved and its practice were indeed compelling reasons for Beck and his colleagues to seek a new approach to treatment.

Unsurprisingly, CBT has been greeted with hostility and as an "upstart" therapy, threatening the comfortable livings of traditional psychoanalysts. In the circumstances it is predictable that psychoanalysis and psychoanalytic psychotherapy are now dirty words to many CBT practitioners despite the fact that the two treatments share many common features, the most obvious being the fact that the patient is treated by the use of words as distinct from drugs or electroconvulsive therapy. CBT was originally the brainchild of Aaron Beck. Beck originally trained as a psychoanalyst in the 1950s (www.beckinstituteblog.org). His first book was published in the 1970s at a time when psychoanalysis (in the United States primarily in the form of ego psychology) was being toppled from its pedestal as the cure for all mental illness. The pedestal it was perched upon was particularly precarious because it aspired to offering a panacea for almost all the problems of the mentally ill in addition to those of the worried well.

Another reason for change was the growth of a demand for evidence of the efficacy of the treatment on offer. From now on, neither the speculation without proof (typical of the writing of Freud and his followers on the one hand), nor clinical pragmatism on the other, would be tolerated unless they could be "proven" to be effective. There were political, social and economic considerations driving this view as well as increasing dissatisfaction with the theories and treatments then available for depression and other mental illnesses.

The economic crises of the 1970s brought into sharp focus the cost of welfare and especially the cost of providing medical care. Over-optimistic claims of the medical establishment had never materialised and despite spiralling costs, disease and human misery continued to prevail in societies that had become used to demanding more. The spiralling costs resulted in a concerted effort to reduce spending. In the USA, health care management examined ways and means of cutting the costs of provision of medical care. Insurance companies and governments were reluctant to foot the bill for the insatiable demand created and maintained by the health care industry, a demand which people had come to see as a right. The demand for empirical evidence regarding the claims of efficacy thus came to exist not just as a means of re-examining the range of treatments on offer but as a means to curtail spending and to ensure that limited resources were spent in a much more cost-effective way. As Hale concludes, "All the unresolved problems of psychotherapy research and of the cost and effectiveness of psychoanalysis raised the issue of insurance cover for psychiatric services" (Hale, 1995, p. 341).

In this environment, the stage was set for other forms of therapy, most notably cognitive behavioural therapies, to emerge. They laid claim to the ground previously dominated by psychoanalysis in the USA by responding to the twin challenges of cost reduction and increase in efficiency. The era of evidence-based, time-limited and cost-effective interventions had begun and CBT had taken the lead. Britain, despite the difference in health care systems, followed a similar path since its government was also unable to fund the ever-increasing demands of health care through taxation.

Moving from the 1970s to the 1980s, there were other changes taking place. Reagan came into power in the USA heading a neo-conservative Republican party and similarly in Britain, Thatcher headed a reinvigorated and triumphant conservative party. Together, they symbolised the return to liberal economics and a shift towards the notion of society not as a unit but a mere collection of individuals. As Thatcher famously remarked, "There is no such thing as society". The "bread crumb" theory dominated: so long as there was plenty of food on the table for the masters, the mice would have enough crumbs to gorge on. Thus there was nothing to complain about. Individuals had seen their standards of living improve, but satisfaction did not improve proportionately. Individuals became more driven by selfish self-interest and the broader long-term good of society was relegated to the back seat. Capitalism and scientific empiricism became the dominant forces in the life of societies. The discourse of capitalism coupled with the discourse of scientific empiricism ensured the collapsing of any space in which their hegemony could be challenged.

It is in this historical context that CBT came to dominate the therapeutic scene and become one of the most influential therapeutic interventions of our time. If the breeding ground for its creation was provided in the 1960s and 1970s, it took the economic conditions and materialism of the 1980s for it to flourish. CBT does not challenge capitalism or recognise the ways in which the latter contributes to human misery. By focusing on the individual and locating the source of misery in structures of the individual mind, capitalism was redeemed.

With its time-limited and scientific empirical stance, it fitted in well with the dominant discourse of the time. The triumph of CBT is not merely the triumph of human rationality and the scientific project. It is the triumph of a particular type of capitalism and scientific empiricism and a treatment that has espoused and encouraged these values. CBT is now well established in many parts of the world, including, Europe and North America, holding a prominent and dominant position in clinical research, as well as clinical practice (Rachman, 1997, p. 3–4).

Rachman (1997) described three stages in the evolution of cognitive behavioural therapy.

1. The first stage (1950–1970s), saw the emergence of behavioural therapy as a prominent treatment modality;
2. In the second stage, the 1960s, cognitive therapy mainly in the USA, was developed;
3. The third stage saw the merging of behavioural therapy and cognitive therapy, a process which gathered momentum in the late 1980s, to form what is now known as CBT.

## Stage 1: The emergence of Behavioural Therapy (BT)

Behavioural Therapy as a psychological treatment emerged around the same time in the USA and the UK, albeit independently. The influences on both groups were somewhat different as were their preoccupations at the time. In the UK, psychologists concentrated on the treatment of neurotic disorders using behavioural approaches. They were influenced by the ideas of Pavlov, Watson and Hull and research work conducted by Wolpe and Eysenck. Eysenck headed the largest graduate psychology department in the UK and his work provided a firm theoretical structure and rationale for Behavioural Therapy, one of the forerunners of CBT. He encouraged research and teaching of behaviour therapy at the Institute of Psychiatry,

London, one of the most important research and training institutions for psychiatry in the UK. Consequently Eysenck had a profound influence on the future of behaviour therapy in Britain (Rachman, 1997, p. 4).

In the USA, psychologists were also influenced by the ideas of B.F. Skinner. Skinner is remembered for his famous experiments where he taught rats how to find their way through mazes as fast as possible. Stimuli, usually in the form of food, had to be offered judiciously; too often and the rats were not hungry enough to bother with the maze; too rarely and they were in danger of giving up because the rewards were not worth the amount of effort (and exercise) involved. Coincidentally at this time, psychoanalysis, American style, offered little in the way of stimuli since practitioners were trained to be impassive, offering as few stimuli as possible. Conversely, but not necessarily contradictorily, it could be argued that visiting your analyst several times a week offered too much stimulation. The patient did not need to do any "homework" herself but she did need to spend lots of time and money "working through" her problems and either way, nothing happened to change her mental state for long periods of time. Skinner and his followers believed that abnormal behaviours could be reshaped through the use of "reinforcement strategies" which encouraged normal behaviours. Unlike their counterparts in the UK, they focused on institutionalised, chronic psychiatric patients who had been deemed untreatable by the psychiatric establishment (Rachman, 1997, p. 5–6).

However, in addition to these differences there were some other crucial divergences between the developments in BT taking place on both sides of the Atlantic. The British, favouring a mixed approach, embraced a qualified environmentalism but more importantly acknowledged the role of biological factors and genetics in the role of psychiatric disorders. In the USA, however, "unqualified environmentalism" was espoused. Behaviour therapists in the USA rejected the role of biological mechanisms and the concepts of "psychiatric disorders" and "abnormal behaviour" were redefined as "problem behaviours". Interestingly, both conventional psychiatric and psychological practice and research were reluctant to take on board the implications of the critique of medical labelling of this kind developed in France by Michel Foucault (for example Foucault, 2006 [1972]). To this day, the same reluctance persists.

Experimental research using behavioural methods and employing animal models provided the evidence that behavioural techniques could be used to modify fears and other abnormal behaviours. Such experimental research provided the empirical basis for theories underpinning behavioural therapies, which had explanatory power regarding the origin of abnormal behaviours, the maintenance of such behaviours, as well as providing the rationale for treatment interventions. The rather significant issue that alone amongst animals, human beings use language in an extremely complex way was largely ignored as was the related fact that language itself influenced behaviour.

With confidence increasing in the methods of Behavioural Therapy (BT) and its empirical support on both sides of the Atlantic, Behavioural Therapists started challenging the dominant force of psychoanalysis, arguing that it lacked any sound empirical basis. BT thus became defined not simply on the basis of what it was; it was also characterised by what it was *not*, in this case, primarily psychoanalytic psychotherapies. Both in the USA and the UK attempts were made to apply what had now become a credible "behavioural science" to a wide range of psychiatric and psychological problems.

The legitimacy of BT, with its foundations in academic-scientific psychology was a significant factor in the insistence on maintaining empirical standards. Psychology, which previously had been limited to carrying out assessments and measurements, was able to advance as a result of the establishment of BT, becoming the distinct profession of clinical psychology.

However, the links with academic psychology, whence BT had originated, gradually disappeared. Whereas significant practical progress had been made in the development of treatments, the interest in theory-building declined, resulting in a shift from conceptualising BT as a science to promulgating it as a technology.

## Stage 2: The emergence of Cognitive Therapy (CT)

By the 1970s, BT had become an established modality of treatment with demonstrable success, particularly in the treatment of anxiety disorders. However, this success was not matched in the treatment of depression and psychosis. Interest in other forms of treatment increased. The resistance to the use of cognitive concepts waned probably, as a consequence of a shift in the intellectual milieu of the time in which behavioural and cognitive approaches were not seen as antithetical to each other but complementary and closely related. Gradually the use of cognitive approaches with behavioural therapy began to demonstrate some success. Beck himself (Beck, Rush, Shaw and Emery, 1979) provides a historical perspective to cognitive models, tracing its philosophical origins back to the Stoic philosophers and including a diverse, and impressive range of theorists, philosophers and practitioners including contemporary contributors from the behavioural and cognitive camp. However, his account fails to give an historical account as to how the influence of such diverse individuals resulted in the development of his specific ideas or indeed the ideas central to CT.

The underpinning rationale of Beck's cognitive therapy is the following proposition: the way the individual feels and behaves is largely contingent upon how he/she structures the world. The challenge for therapy was, therefore, to find ways of identifying faulty cognitions, to enable reality testing and subsequently to correct the underlying distorted conceptualisations and dysfunctional beliefs that were causing affective and behavioural disturbance. The crucial shift here was the linking of thoughts, emotions and behaviours in a cognitive system, within which cognitions had primacy. The therapy was therefore directed at correcting these faulty cognitions and, instead of concentrating on historical issues, it focused on present problems and present thinking patterns. In addition to a range of cognitive techniques, Beck later incorporated a range of behavioural techniques (see below), although he regarded them as being of secondary value in changing faulty cognitions.

Around the same time as Beck was experimenting with early versions of CBT, Ellis came up with similar ideas, emphasising the role of cognitions in emotional and psychological disturbance. He believed that emotional and psychological disturbance resulted from irrational and illogical thinking, which could be addressed by minimising illogical thinking and maximising rational thinking. Although the contributions of Ellis have been widely recognised, it is Beck's version that has provided the main thrust for the development of cognitive therapy and its dominant position in today's world.

Beck's initial writings focused on the treatment of depression and it was only later that the principles of cognitive therapy were applied to other mental disorders. Beck's analysis of depression is described in detail in the next chapter. In brief, according to Beck's cognitive formulation of depression, depressed individuals are engaged in faulty information processing and reasoning, subscribing to self-defeating schemas. This entails a negative view of oneself, the world and the future. Interventions by therapists should be delivered in a structured and time-limited manner, focusing on correcting these errors of thinking and thus breaking the self-perpetuating cycle and enabling the individual to get out of this bleak space.

## Stage 3: The merging of Behavioural and Cognitive Therapy approaches and the emergence of CBT

The development of cognitive therapy took place at a time when psychology as a discipline was already strongly moving in the direction of cognitive theories and explanations. However, these two developments occurred quite separately from each other and, beyond their overall general outlook, there is little more than superficial similarity between the two, especially in terms of their underpinning theories, terminology and methodologies. Cognitive psychology assumed that the majority of cognitive processing was not consciously accessible, in contrast to cognitive therapy, which tended to focus almost exclusively on consciously experienced thoughts and images. Most of the techniques of the latter therefore aimed at dealing with conscious thoughts and their subsequent correction. Nevertheless, with the exception of some concerns, the development of cognitive therapy was welcomed and its inclusion of behavioural techniques perhaps resulted in a degree of acceptance, or at least less resistance, from the behavioural therapists. The imprecise use of the term "cognition" and its development independently and, at times, in contradiction to academic research in psychology, gave them cause for some concern.

With an overall shift towards cognitive psychology, cognitive concepts became accepted and gradually acquired a prominent position within psychology. Psychology has traditionally focussed on experimentation and the use of animal models in laboratory-based research. A gradual dissatisfaction with the claims of psychology to be a behavioural science arose. Its concerns were viewed as somewhat detached from human experience and behaviour. It was in this context that the merging of BT and CT could become possible and indeed took place. This resulted in a successful treatment for panic disorder being developed, incorporating techniques and theoretical insights from both forms of treatment. BT brought its focus on empiricism and scientific integrity, a focus that still remains a prominent feature of CBT.

The coming together of these two forms of treatment had its own set of practical, as well as conceptual problems. However, through an exchange of ideas they were able to provide more sophisticated models for understanding a range of disorders. Cognitive concepts were incorporated into behavioural treatments and behavioural experiments were incorporated in cognitive treatments, potentially for the better. Crucially, CBT thus formed, imbued its practitioners with confidence and optimism. Treatments for a range of psychiatric disorders based on CBT were developed, with clear underpinning theoretical models, sophisticated formulations and targeted interventions. The practitioners also engaged enthusiastically in research providing the scientific evidence establishing CBT as an empirically derived treatment with empirical evidence of its efficacy, unrivalled by any other form of psychological treatment.

Today the CBT lobby occupies a strong position. It emphasises its own scientific credentials in relation to other therapeutic endeavours; rival therapies are edged out on the grounds that they have not been able to acquire the "legitimacy" of being regarded as a scientific enterprise. The hegemony of scientific discourse is maintained as is the power of groups such as CBT practitioners in relation to others. This is also of importance for financial reasons.

Using the UK as an example, the current Improving Access to Psychological Therapies (IAPT) is a government initiative to provide brief CBT interventions for workers who are off sick—ostensibly with anxiety and depression—in an endeavour to treat them quickly and enable them to return to work before the situation becomes less amenable to change. IAPT resulted from a report submitted by Lord Layard regarding the loss of economic productivity as a result of depression. Layard's brief report highlighted the economic effect of the loss to the economy of up to 1 in 6 workers who, at some time in their lives, will take time off work because of depression and related conditions.

The IAPT project has had a huge impact on another British government initiative, the Agenda for Change. The Agenda for Change is the reformed salary structure in the NHS which links rates of pay to the nature and complexity of work undertaken. Those who supervise and manage others receive higher salaries and those who focus mainly on delivering interventions receive less. Psychologists in particular have acquired a powerful position in relation to other groups. They are the dominant professional group, by virtue of their training, regarded as qualified to deliver empirical therapies such as CBT, as well as supervising other practitioners delivering such interventions. This translates into occupational stability and ensures increased levels of financial remuneration for psychologists.

Within the mental health establishment traditionally, power had resided with psychiatry, to a certain extent reflecting traditional class structures where the medical professionals mainly come from the middle classes. Psychology, a profession similarly middle-class in its outlook, has challenged this power base. Thus a reframing of individual problems is being formulated through the alternative psychological cognitive-behavioural framework, instead of from a biomedical point of view. A shift in the frame, presented as a progression from the "primitive" medical frameworks to the more "democratic" (people want more talking therapies) demonstrates how socio-cultural currents can be used to bring about shifts in prevailing power structures. Whether there is any difference insofar as the individual is concerned remains to be seen.

In theory, the much-criticised patriarchy of medicine is gradually being replaced by a more "humane" CBT. Contrary to popular perception, the latter in fact closely adheres to the central tenets of patriarchy. The distressed individual is first of all told that their way of thinking is wrong and then they are told how to correct their "flaws in thinking" in accordance with the empirical model of CBT. Overall, a more nuanced discussion as to why a psychological as opposed to a medical framework might be more appropriate is conspicuously lacking. There is an even more interesting question: why is the CBT model more appropriate than a sociological understanding of the societal origin of many individual difficulties? Or indeed, why are other possible frameworks for understanding contemporary malaise excluded from mainstream discourse?

Another dimension of the exercising of power is observable in the context of training in clinical psychology. The latter are now the dominant provider of CBT training in the UK. Generally speaking, trainees are accepted into membership when they are deemed to be ready; in most professions this is a byword for the point in time when their views start conforming to generally accepted norms within the profession. Clinical psychology and CBT are no exception. Individuals whose views conform not only find it easier to be accepted for training; they are also better placed to progress. Those who fail to conform are sidelined. It is not so much the case that dissenting professionals cannot exist, but rather that they become less able to influence mainstream thoughts and thinking from within. In this way the structure preserves its dominance through stamping out or discouraging dissent beyond certain fixed limits.

At this point we turn our attention to a more detailed account of how CBT works in its current form.

## CHAPTER TWO

# What is cognitive behavioural therapy and what does it claim to do?

The situation in which Beck found himself was one where people were discouraged and cynical. Psychoanalysis American-style did not work—or at least it did not deliver the answers demanded by a country, which was one of the leading engines of capitalism. Patients went to see their analysts because they were miserable and they remained miserable. Beck was scathing about this situation. Rather than simply accept the implicit message of American psychoanalysis, viz, the work of analysis is to allow the patient time to shave off the corners of the awkward square pegs of their personalities in order that they fit into round holes created by society, Beck reasoned—why not actively stimulate this process instead of waiting for something to change?

Using Beck's new approach to therapy, patients were encouraged to formulate their problems (emotional, behavioural and physiological) as resulting from negative thoughts. The therapist, having educated the client in the basic theory underpinning CBT, then enabled the patient to see that the negative thoughts and perceptions were crippling her emotional life and that they could be replaced by thoughts based on a more realistic appraisal of her situation using an empirical approach. "Homework" was central to reinforcing insights gained in therapy sessions but also, by making the patient practise activities which gave shape to her day, organizing her thinking, and taking up "mind" space that might otherwise dwell for too long on the negative aspects of her experience, it broke up the vicious cycle of negativity. It is interesting that the patients whom Beck treated initially seem to have come from a group of reasonably well-off women much like those who had turned to psychoanalysis in the early days of Freud's practice (e.g., Beck, 1976, p. 38). They were women who were often financially supported by men, who often had young families to look after but for whom society only offered very limited opportunities to become career women, let alone the main breadwinner for a family. Initially CBT seems to have been aimed at a section of the population who are often described as "the worried well". Since then, CBT has been offered to a much wider range of people to the extent that the layman is often invited by the media if not necessarily by proponents of CBT, to view the treatment as a panacea for all mental illnesses.

As we indicated above, other cognitive therapeutic approaches have been devised. There are other forms of CBT most notably Young's Schema Focused Therapy, as well as many modifications of Beck's original Cognitive Therapy. However, Beck's version has been the most influential. Originally he developed Cognitive Therapy for the treatment of depression but since then it has been successfully applied to a range of other psychiatric disorders. As a result, the therapy has often been modified, making use of behavioural approaches and tailoring the model to meet the requirements for treating particular disorders. Specific models have been devised for a wide range of emotional problems. However, although there are differences in the specific treatment models, the overall approach remains fairly similar though understandably with differential emphases.

## Beck's cognitive model of depression

For the sake of brevity, we shall focus on Beck's account of Cognitive Therapy for the treatment of depression in order to provide an understanding of some of the key features of his approach. Beck's cognitive model of depression evolved from his clinical and experimental work, resulting in the development of a model of depression and a therapy based on it. The cognitive model of depression provides an understanding in cognitive terms of what predisposes individuals to become depressed, what precipitates an episode of depression and how such episodes are maintained. It also provides a framework in which cognitions have primacy and explain the symptoms of depression as consequences of faulty cognitions and faulty information processing. This provides the rationale for specific interventions and the basis for treatment. Three specific concepts are introduced to explain the psychological underpinnings of depression:

1. The cognitive triad
2. Schemas
3. Cognitive errors

"The cognitive triad" refers to the cognitive pattern frequently seen in depressed clients. Firstly, depressed individuals tend to hold a negative view of themselves, generally regarding themselves as innately defective and inadequate, as a result of which they see themselves as undesirable and worthless. The second aspect, relating to their negative view of the world is a result of the tendency of depressed individuals to interpret their *ongoing* experience in a negative way, despite evidence to the contrary. The third and final component is a negative view of the *future*. Depressed people expect that their difficulties will continue endlessly, resulting in a sense of hopelessness and helplessness. In cognitive therapy most of the symptoms of depression are seen as stemming from negative cognitions and as a consequence, these produce negative emotions, physiological changes and behaviours.

The cognitive model of depression suggests that early experiences may provide the basis for development of negative "schemas". Schemas refer to the underlying relatively stable cognitive patterns that help individuals organise their experience of life. Schemas enable people to deal with immense amounts of incoming external and internal stimuli encountered in day to day life, by concentrating only on a limited number of stimuli. However, each person's experience of life is, of course, unique. The schemas they have assembled are used to process ordinary everyday situations on the basis of the assumptions previously made. Specific schemas may be activated by specific events under stressful circumstances forming what becomes an ingrained series of attitudes, a lense through which the person views her world. Many schemas may be negative when they hamper the individual's adaptation to her situation although they can be positive when they facilitate a process of constructive adaptation.

These negative schemas can be latent but may be activated by specific external circumstances resulting in automatic thoughts of a negative nature (negative automatic thoughts or NATS) potentially resulting in the development and maintenance of the syndrome of depression. In severe depression, one series of depressing thoughts reinforces and maintains the others, thus locking the client in a vicious circle of self-perpetuating misery. Depressed people deploy these negative schemas perpetuating self-defeating and painful attitudes, despite positive experiences and evidence to the contrary. As the severity of the depression increases, depressogenic schemas indeed become autonomous, acquiring a life of their own independent of the environment and regardless of present circumstances. The emotional, physiological and behavioural responses seen in depression, which stem from the negative thoughts, are products of underlying core beliefs and schemas and are precipitated by specific events reinforcing the underlying negative thoughts, schemas and core beliefs. The individual sinks ever deeper into a mental quagmire, itself a product of their own thoughts.

Early in childhood people develop views regarding themselves, the people around them and the world they inhabit; these views become crystallised into beliefs. Some of these beliefs take the form of "absolute truths" and are so deeply established that they are not even articulated. These beliefs are referred to as "core beliefs" and they are global, rigid and overgeneralised. According to Beck, schemas are intricately linked with core beliefs and arise from the same early childhood experiences. Schemas are relatively enduring cognitive structures that enable individuals to organise their experiences. Perhaps the best way to conceptualise the relationship between core beliefs and schemas is to see schemas as the underlying structure and the core belief as its content (Beck, J; 1995, p. 166). Core beliefs influence the development of an intermediate category of beliefs, consisting of attitudes, rules and assumptions. These again are frequently not articulated but have an impact on how a situation is appraised, which in turn influences how the individual thinks, feels and behaves in any given situation.

"Cognitive errors" are systematic information processing errors frequently seen in people suffering from depression. They maintain the sufferer's underlying belief in the negativity of their thoughts despite the lack of supporting evidence or indeed evidence to the contrary. Arbitrary inference, selective abstraction, over-generalisation, magnification and minimisation, personalisation and dichotomous thinking are typical of the cognitive errors commonly observed.

Thus the cognitive model of depression focuses on the individual; it also takes into account the environment and negative interpersonal experiences that play an important role in the precipitation and maintenance of depression. However, just as the therapy focuses on cognitions rather than emotions and behaviours, it stresses the role of the individual rather than the environment in understanding the causes of depression. It is noteworthy that individuals suffering from depression may often interact with significant others in their life by withdrawing, thus increasing their own experience of alienation, sense of rejection and self-criticism; this sets up a vicious cycle that perpetuates the depression. On the other hand a harmonious relationship can be of great benefit in neutralising the individual's negativity, preventing him/her from slipping deeper and helping in a speedy recovery. Moreover, friends and family members acting as "auxiliary therapists" can be taught techniques, mainly in order to facilitate the implementation of cognitive and behavioural therapeutic interventions in the domestic environment (Beck, Rush, Shaw & Emery, 1979, p. 33).

Up to this point we have laid out the background of theory on which the practice of cognitive therapy was based. In essence, cognitive therapy has been described as "an active, directive, time limited, structured approach used to treat a variety of psychiatric disorders" (Beck, Rush, Shaw & Emery, 1979, p. 3).

In cognitive therapy, although cognitions, emotions and behaviours are all regarded as being important, cognitions are explicitly given primacy. Whereas it could be argued that negative emotions or indeed negative behaviours could result in negative thoughts, in the cognitive model, such arguments are rejected. Instead, emotions and behaviours are considered to be dependent on cognitions further "upstream". If we accept that negative emotions and negative behaviours are the result of negative cognitions, then a reasonable approach would be to tackle the negative cognitions in order to bring about improvements in mood and behaviour. Thus, the following central assumptions underpin the practice of cognitive therapy. People are deemed to actively process perceptual and experiential information from internal and external sources, which gives rise to cognitions (thoughts, images etc). These cognitions form the individual's "stream of consciousness" reflecting his/her conceptualisation of self, the world, the past and the future. Just as important are negative cognitions which are understood to result from cognitive distortions and which can therefore have a corresponding negative impact on the individual's emotions and behaviours. The purpose of CBT is to make the sufferer aware of their cognitive distortions and through cognitive techniques, which are described below, correct the negative distortions in order to achieve positive results.

To summarise, central to Beck's theory is the assumption that the individuals' emotions (affect) and behaviours are dependent on how the individual organises his/her experience of the external or internal world. The importance of cognitions, images and verbal events consciously experienced by the individual is stressed; these are deemed to have primacy over emotions and behaviours. In depression, it is thought that cognitions resulting in disturbance of emotion and behaviour are frequently inaccurate. They are deemed to be the result of faulty information processing. In cognitive therapy, it is the conscious negative image or thought that drives the negative emotion and disturbance of behaviour and therefore the target of therapy is primarily to alter these faulty thoughts or to change the faulty processes that caused the faulty thoughts in the first place. In Beck's account this brief summary is often presented as unproblematic.

In fact, Beck's view of the primacy of cognitions has been challenged by cognitive psychologists in the field. Teasdale disagrees with Beck's view, citing evidence that, whereas negative cognitions can result in depressed mood, depressed mood can also result in negative cognitions. He suggests instead that in reality it is far more likely that they have a reciprocal impact on each other. He goes further and asserts that apparently similar mood states can have different effects on cognitions and indeed apparently related cognitions can have diverse effects on emotions. He therefore concludes that in reality the distinction between cognitions and mood may be far from clear (Teasdale, 1997, p. 67–8).

> ... I shall suggest that, if we are to do justice those complexities, we are forced to frame our analysis beyond the simple level of the effects of thoughts and beliefs on emotion. Rather I will suggest that, particularly in the case of mood disorders such as depression, our analyses have to be at the level of integrated, motivated, patterns of information-processing, that continue over extended periods of time, and that involve multiple levels of information and cognitive representation. (Teasdale, 1997, p. 70)

As indicated in the previous chapter, Beck enhanced the effectiveness of his new approach by using some aspects of the work of B.F. Skinner. Skinner and his followers developed a technique known as operant conditioning, using rats in order to obtain their initial experimental data. Operant conditioning is a means of changing behaviour by utilising reinforcement strategies. Good behaviour is reinforced by the offer of a small reward; aberrant behaviour is discouraged by some kind of mild punishment. Whereas Behavioural Therapists believed that such reinforcement schedules in their own right were sufficient to bring about behavioural change, CBT practitioners were of the view that behavioural experiments provided real data for clients and therapists to use in the service of altering underlying negative cognitions, as well as acting as a reinforcer.

Thus for an individual with depression who has become socially withdrawn, with the underlying negative thought that nobody would want to be with somebody like him/her, the therapist may in collaboration with the patient set up a behavioural experiment e.g., for the patient to spend some time, mutually agreed by therapist and patient, with a friend or family member. When in the depths of misery, this encounter in its own right may provide a welcome reprieve from the internal torment for the patient, thus making it more likely for such behaviour to be repeated, rendering the patient less isolated and withdrawn. From a CBT point of view, such an interchange provides valuable data; the therapist is then in a position to get the patient to examine the data that this experiment generates to challenge the underlying negative thought ("nobody would want to be with somebody like me"), replacing it with a more realistic version based on the evidence provided by the experiment. This process seeks to replace the previous negative thought, and therefore the negative down stream effects on emotions, physiological responses and behaviours. At the same time, it probably reduces the possibility of the patient slipping back into daydreaming negative thoughts.

Patients are asked to go home and carry out certain activities and to monitor and challenge their negative thoughts. They are further encouraged to organise their lives by carrying out tasks at fixed times as agreed with the therapist. The activities may be very concrete ones such as loading the dishwasher each morning before leaving the house, playing the piano for a fixed length of time or a more complex and less concrete task such as meeting someone for lunch. An interesting and typical feature of this example of CBT is that the patient is encouraged *to do* things. This is a far cry from the much more passive stance of both therapist and patient in psychoanalytic styles of therapy. Actions by the patient are used to reinforce the message of the therapy that positive thoughts can overcome negative ones.

## Development of the personality

Beck and his colleagues adopted a Darwinian evolutionary approach towards personality development. They suggest that individuals are endowed with genetically-determined strategies. As a result of the process of natural selection, those strategies favouring survival and reproduction became dominant. Thus individuals demonstrate "programmed" behaviours that are genetically determined. These programmes involve cognitive processing, affect, action, self-regulation and motivation and have gradually evolved to become ever more efficient over thousands of generations.

However, CBT is not a purely biological theory. Human beings are not yet a species of living robots. Genetically-determined programmes are regarded as innate predispositions, which interact with the external environment. The latter in turn influences the development of schemas (Pretzer and Beck, 1996). These schemas are thought to be relatively stable cognitive structures which have developed as a means of organising experiences and which are part of normal cognitive development. Patterns of behaviour or strategies are related to cognitive, affective, motivational, action and self-regulatory schemas (Davidson, 2000, p. 17). Schemas influence automatic processes such as perception, affective and action responses. In order for the strategies to be realised, genetic endowment is, on its own, insufficient to account for the highly personal and often unpredictable response of different individuals to very common experiences such as loss and bereavement. It is only through an interaction with the environment that the genetic endowment can manifest itself as a strategy in specific situations. The individual's experience, both of the environment and other people, results in the some schemas becoming over-developed and others being minimised. In mental disorders what we see is an exaggerated form of these otherwise normal primitive strategies.

This brief summary is largely congruent with the neo-Darwinian accounts of the relationship between consciousness and the brain produced by contemporary philosophers such as Daniel Dennett (e.g., see Dennett, 1991). For the purposes of this book, it is worth recording the fact that Dennett's view has been both challenged and elaborated by philosophers and psychologists such as Stephen Jay Gould, Merlin Donald and Nicholas Humphrey: suffice it to say that all would agree that the relationship between mind/brain/consciousness and evolution is to say the least complicated!

Cognitive therapy incorporated some new and distinctive features, emphasising its difference from other therapies, particularly the psychoanalytic psychotherapies, and stressing its empirical basis. According to Beck, Rush, Shaw and Emery, cognitive therapy offered the following new features:

1. Collaborative empiricism;
2. Focus on the "here and now";
3. Emphasis on empirical investigation. (Beck, Rush, Shaw & Emery 1979).

Collaborative empiricism refers to the joint endeavour of therapist and client, with the explicit aim of examining (using a scientific approach) the evidence for or against underlying thoughts and beliefs. The focus on the "here and now" was originally in part a reaction to the phenomenon of "dredging the past"—a feature of many forms of psychoanalytic psychotherapies. In the latter there was a focus on the past, sometimes to the exclusion of the present and the future. A feature which cognitive therapists often emphasized was the use of empirical investigation as a tool of treatment. The cognitive therapist's task was to enable the client to become a scientist who would examine his/her own perceptions, thoughts and experiences using scientific principles. Scientific empiricism became firmly rooted not only in the underpinning theory but in the actual clinical practice of cognitive therapy.

In the light of this complex philosophical and theoretical background, Beck adopted a pragmatic approach to the development of CBT as a therapy. He concentrated on developing his ideas regarding the treatment of depression and other disorders by emphasising the role played by our cognitions in determining how we lead our lives. CBT therefore is modelled on the idea that patients are suffering from disorders, which can be measured using an instrument such as the Beck

Depression Inventory (BDI) (briefly described in chapter three). The main focus of CBT is on its role in the clinic. This approach has been at the expense of a clear theoretical exposition of a cognitive model of normal development. The latter could provide a comparison with the development of psychopathology in the individual. However, Beck appears to have been more interested in producing an account, albeit speculative in nature, which possessed some scientific credibility and which was internally coherent for the application of cognitive techniques.

When Beck and his colleagues turned their attention to personality disorders, then the need to address this gap in the model—at least partially—became clear. When depression is measured by a questionnaire such as the BDI, depression is, in a sense, self-reporting. In the case of personality disorder, however, it is up to the clinician to assess whether a patient suffers from this condition. In many cases the sufferer would be unable to self-report, precisely because one of the aspects of this condition is that the patient has a very poor understanding of the reasons for his own behaviour. Any treatment of personality disorder requires some kind of definition of the nature of the disorder so that the clinician can look for signs when making a diagnosis and assessment of such conditions.

Beck's cognitive account of personality is rather unclear; the nearest he gets to defining what might be regarded as "personality", is to suggest that it is characterised by a range of schemas that in the course of the individual's development, have become "prominent". Beck's theory runs as follows:

1. There is an initial deployment of strategies in relation to specific situational demands;
2. These strategies are dependent on information processing through underlying schemas;

3. The underlying schemas are relatively stable underlying cognitive structures that help the individual to organise his/her experience;
4. In response to specific situational demands, influenced by underlying schemas, individuals will evaluate the situation;
5. This results in emotional and motivational arousal and subsequent deployment of strategies in the form of behaviours. (Beck, Freeman & Davis, 2004, p. 17–18).

The role of schemas in the deployment of strategies is central and, according to the cognitive model, these schemas are regarded as the fundamental unit of personality, on which the individual's cognitive, emotional and motivational processes depend. Personality traits are then merely overt expressions of these underlying structures. With regard to normal personality development, it is a matter of the individual having an environment that interacts with his/her biologically determined predispositions to produce more reality-oriented, adaptive schemas. A lack of "fit" between the individual's innate predispositions could potentially result in the development of less adaptive and dysfunctional schemas and consequently result in psychopathology that might attract labels such as "mental disorder" or "personality disorder".

Beck's account is of course speculative and to a certain extent it sounds plausible. However, it prompts questions for the following reasons:

1. It is fairly clear that his theory is in fact a theory of psychopathology;
2. Thus "normality" is at best vague and at worst portrayed simply as the absence of psychopathology;
3. CBT assumes that human beings are primarily sophisticated machines. Our brains are conceived of as sophisticated computers which exist to process information. If human beings

have to be persuaded to be rational using CBT, then why are they dysfunctional to begin with?

4. Who decides what constitutes dysfunctional behaviour? In Foucault's *History of Madness* (2006 [1972]), Foucault demonstrates that cognitions that are deemed to be dysfunctional are heavily dependent upon the prevailing cultural ethos of the day—a Darwinian evolutionary model might be part of the story but leaves out this crucial component;

5. Foucault charts the spectacular changes in thinking about what he calls "Unreason" rather than madness or dysfunctional behaviour. Even today, neither CBT nor other medical models of illness offer us reasons *why* people are sad, delusional, terrified of living or any other of the hundreds of symptoms that constitute being diagnosed dysfunctional or mentally ill;

6. Beck also struggles to make a case for the distinction listed in DSM IV between Axis-1 and Axis-2 disorders. The Psychiatric classificatory system used in the USA, the DSM-IV (American Psychiatric Association 1994) employs a multiaxial diagnostic system. It has 5 axes; Axis-1 is for coding of major psychiatric disorders such as schizophrenia, major depression, bipolar affective disorder etc, Axis-2 is to code for the presence of personality disorders and Axes-3, -4 and -5 allow for the coding of the presence of medical conditions, social conditions and overall levels of functioning. These take up the weak argument of rigidity, pervasiveness and lack of flexibility for Axis-2 and the episodic nature of Axis-1 disorders though the debateable assumption that the whole spectrum of personality and personality traits occur on a continuum.

7. Beck's theories do not conform to the realities found in the clinic for the following reasons:
   a) Individuals with depression have been shown to have underlying dysfunctional schemas even when they have recovered;

b)   Furthermore, individuals who have personality disorders also have periods (when not confronted by overwhelming external stressors) when they are able to function relatively well with an episodic pattern relating to their symptoms and levels of functioning.

## The practice of CBT

So what might CBT in practice look like? Here is an example. A patient B is suffering from depression. She has become socially withdrawn and isolated, spending increasing amounts of time in bed, consumed with negativity and guilt. The CBT practitioner, following a thorough assessment, enters into an agreement with the patient, about which areas to tackle first. Initially this may take the form of encouraging the patient to get out of bed in the morning, get dressed and feed herself (sometimes known as activity scheduling). The therapist may then ask the patient to keep a diary of her thoughts and feelings (the daily thought record) as well as establishing with the patient the underlying negative thoughts precipitating her negative feelings. Patient B may not wish to see anyone due to a negative thought such as, "Nobody would want to be with someone as miserable as me". The therapist enables B to examine the evidence for and against this thought, replacing it with a more realistic version closer to reality and therefore potentially less distressing to B. Errors in how the patient appraises the evidence are highlighted (cognitive distortions) and behavioural experiments may be set up to check out whether people would or would not want to spend time with the patient. Thus the capacity of B (and many patients like her) to use their logical thought-processes and capabilities for rational thinking is harnessed to enable a quick and effective cure for what is a crippling problem. There are some essential preconditions for such work. B's negative thoughts have to be identified and clearly separated from her positive thoughts.

The process assumes that various conditions apply or can be made to apply:

- The negative aspects of the patient's life must be capable of being clearly separated from the potential positive aspects;
- The patient must be sufficiently intelligent to follow the distinction between rational and irrational forms of thinking;
- The patient must not be in the throes of a hallucinatory psychosis, characterised by an inability to distinguish external reality from internal thoughts in the mind.

In order to achieve the aims of cognitive therapy, a number of techniques have been devised. In order for them to work, it is considered important that they are deployed within the cognitive model's conceptual framework of depression. Theoretical knowledge of the cognitive model is considered to be of importance and indeed, in the first few sessions of therapy, introducing the framework underpinning CBT is an integral part of the therapy itself. Therapeutic techniques are designed to identify the client's distorted cognitions and underlying faulty thoughts, otherwise known as "dysfunctional beliefs". Once the dysfunctional beliefs have been identified in the therapy, techniques are used to enable the individual to test for herself the validity of her thoughts. Eventually she will be able to correct some of these erroneous cognitions and beliefs. Clients often believe that their faulty beliefs are in fact true, even if there is substantial evidence to the contrary. In a sense, cognitive therapy problematises the ideas that the client brings to the therapy claiming to be facts or truths about her life, rather than accepting them at face value. Instead, through adopting a stance of scientific enquiry, the therapist enables the client to challenge some of these erroneous conclusions and beliefs, with consequent improvement in mood and behaviour.

In CBT language then, specific situations are influenced by the individual's core beliefs, schemas, and intermediate beliefs (attitudes, rules and assumptions). Individuals have automatic thoughts, which in turn influence the individual's emotions and behaviours. If the automatic thoughts are of a negative nature, they are termed "negative automatic thoughts" (NATS). NATS result in negative emotions, as well as influencing the individual's behaviour and often lead to a physiological response. NATS are the focus of most of the initial interventions in cognitive therapy and can result in significant improvement in mood and behaviours.

The whole approach of cognitive therapy is geared towards enabling the client to acquire techniques, which they can use in the absence of the therapist, to challenge problematic thoughts. Focusing on the specific learning experience of the client, cognitive therapy approaches are designed to teach the client:

1. Monitoring of negative automatic thoughts (NATS);
2. Recognition of connections between cognitions, affects and behaviours;
3. Examination of evidence for and against habitual thoughts;
4. Replacing biased interpretations with more balanced ones;
5. Identification and altering of dysfunctional beliefs, which predispose to distorted experience.

In cognitive therapy, the therapist listens to the client's account of their difficulties, paying attention not only to the account but also to links between cognitions, affects and behaviours as well as underlying beliefs. Various verbal techniques are used to explore the basis for specific cognitions and assumptions and this helps the therapist to generate an initial tentative hypothesis in cognitive terms, regarding the nature of the individual's problems and how best to approach them. The client is then given a rationale for cognitive therapy, thus introducing the client to the model and its workings. The client is also introduced to some of the tools that they will be using in the course of therapy. Initially the client is asked to maintain a "Daily Record of Dysfunctional Thought", which facilitates the recognition and monitoring of troublesome thoughts through active recording. This also provides fruitful data for discussions in future therapy sessions. Therapy is explicitly focused on specific target symptoms agreed between therapist and client. Associated cognitions are identified and subjected to logical and empirical investigation. The therapist with the client examines the cognitions and underlying assumptions brought up in the Daily Record for:

1. Logic
2. Validity
3. Adaptiveness
4. Enhancement of positive behaviour versus maintenance of pathology.

From a learning-model perspective, sessions in cognitive therapy act as a learning experience and the client gradually starts to incorporate into their own thinking the therapeutic techniques and interventions used by the therapist. In essence, the client gradually starts using the same techniques in between sessions and, in so doing, gains some mastery over situations previously regarded as beyond his/her control. The role of behavioural techniques is explicitly acknowledged in cognitive therapy. In fact, for the more severely depressed, cognitive therapy advocates the use of behavioural techniques to help bring about change. Behavioural techniques in the form of behavioural experiments are conceptualised as part of the empirical venture, generating important cognitive information that can be empirically examined in sessions and, at the same time, testing the validity of beliefs and conclusions. Sessions with the client provide the opportunity for both client and therapist to hypothesise about the original nature of the difficulties experienced by the individual. This is a dynamic process and client and therapist should continue to re-evaluate the conceptualisation aiming to refine it and using it to target interventions in the most effective way.

Not all CBT therapy is conducted face to face. *Beating the Blues*® is a recent attempt by an NHS-backed private company, Ultrasis, to provide CBT via a computer programme directly to the consumer. The website informs us that it is the result of a joint project between a private company and the Institute of Psychiatry. Apparently *Beating the Blues*® has been "scientifically proven". It claims to alleviate depression and anxiety. However, buried in the legal disclaimer we find this:

- The Goods and Services are not intended for use in diagnosing or treating medical or psychiatric conditions, and are not a substitute for fully qualified professional medical or psychiatric advice and should not be treated as such. If you are actively considering self-harm or suicide, or suffer from any other serious mental disorder such as but not excluding psychosis, bipolar disease, dementia or personality disorder, then you should consider seeking qualified medical advice.
- It is the User's responsibility at all times to seek appropriate help if they are actively considering self harm or suicide during their use of the Goods and Services. (www. ultrasis.com)

This computerised CBT programme can be purchased on payment of £30 for screening (over the telephone?) and then a further payment of £295. A reasonable assumption from consulting the website is that it *may* be offered free if your GP purchases it for you. The accompanying video on the website shows a successful user who claims to have had extensive (if useless) therapeutic help for many years. The assumption we are invited to make is that she no longer suffers from any of the mental health problems she experienced before using the computer programme. Either the user, or of course in some cases the GP, are assumed to be in a position to "know" whether or not a potential user's anxiety and depression can be safely separated from a host of conditions (each of which of course may well *in themselves* produce anxiety and depression in spades) before signing up to this programme.

The above is a brief account of what CBT sets out to do and how it works. In the next chapter we shall look at the evidence relating to CBT. We shall address issues relating to the quality of its evidence base and discuss its effectiveness in comparison with other treatments.

## CHAPTER THREE

# The status of cognitive behavioural therapy as a scientific treatment

This chapter sets out a series of detailed arguments about Cognitive Behavioural Therapy's claim to be "scientific" and "evidence-based". Many critics of CBT focus on the ethical, moral and philosophical issues surrounding its practice in contradistinction to other kinds of therapies. We will not neglect these issues, but unlike most commentators, we will also discuss the evidence put forward by researchers who have assessed CBT's claims to efficacy over the years. Also included in this chapter is a brief overview of the ongoing discussion between The British Psychological Society and Skills for Health in creating National Occupational Standards for CBT. This debate highlights some of the problems of delivering CBT as a scientific treatment.

If you keep up with coverage of health topics in the media, you might think that the only ways we have of thinking about mental health and the emotional lives of people are either via numbers, presented as part of a research project involving statistics or by the discovery of a new gene for x. These are both fashionable ways of thinking, although there are, in fact, other well-established possibilities for discovering information about human experience. Many commentators have criticised

CBT from the perspective of claiming that rival treatments are more humane, more ethical or simply more effective. Others have commented on the manifold problems of establishing credible scientific evidence relating to the whole range of psychotherapies whilst in broad terms supporting the drive to improve their evidence base (Roth & Fonagy, 2005). We take an extremely brief overview here of both approaches.

## Philosophical arguments

Traditionally in the UK we have preferred to focus on what's wrong with the individual and provide solutions to problems within this framework rather than examining the conflictual issues of society generally, of which the problems of individuals can be viewed as mere manifestations, for which more radical solutions may be required. CBT focuses on the individual as opposed to the collective. This is very much in line with most approaches of our time. However, the question nevertheless remains as to why this should be the case. If the spotlight is on the individual, and attribution of rationality and responsibility is to the individual alone, then the collective abdicates its responsibility for the injustices and misery of society. Furthermore, revealing questions about the kind of society we wish to live in and how our current actions facilitate or hinder such a project are left untouched. By couching itself as a treatment, these questions are side-stepped; at the same time CBT helps maintain the current order of the social fabric. As Foucault demonstrates, medical, psychological and social interventions are all inherently political with repercussions for both present and future society. Currently the government prefers the view that the causes of day-to-day problems that people experience are to be located in the ills of the education system or the health system. The idea that the underlying cause is poverty or indeed any other social problem is now unfashionable. Unsurprisingly, however, the credit crunch is prompting a revival of interest in questioning the current approach.

Here is a recent example. Depression and other mental health problems cause many lost days from work and there is a plethora of evidence which shows that the longer someone is out of work, the less likely they are to find another job. The numbers of people made redundant are rapidly increasing as a result of the credit crunch. The view is therefore adopted that CBT could be used as a form of early intervention so that people don't become depressed; they can then (it is hoped) find jobs and return to work (even though jobs are being lost rapidly) as quickly as possible. There is no suggestion that they have suddenly become mentally ill. However an assumption that underlies this proposal is that misfortunes in life quickly lead to mental illness. Would society sanction the prophylactic use of anti-depressants to ward off illness in the same instance?

This example also provides us with a typical lack of "joined-up" thinking often found in the decisions of British politicians. Quite apart from the benefits or otherwise of CBT it is assumed that jobs will magically become available for those who have been treated. The dubious ethics of raising false hopes have not been considered. This is still the ethics of cut-throat capitalism, where failure to get a job is construed as a failure of the individual to adapt to the contemporary demands for a cheap and flexible workforce.

This is an example of applying a "treatment" without considering the wider issues of whether we are dealing with mental illness here or simply the trials and tribulations of ordinary everyday living. Perhaps this is not important. However, there is an assumption that intervention is automatically "a good thing". Others may see this proposal as yet another example of the "nanny" state. One could even put a more sinister gloss on this by suggesting that it is the beginnings of the slippery slope of a coercive approach to those who are out of work. Will the next move be to punish those who refuse CBT by reducing their benefits—the negative reinforcement which worked so well with Skinner's rats? If unemployment produces large numbers of people who need treatment, this raises questions about the arbitrary way in which we draw the lines between health and illness.

Despite the slippage in distinguishing between redundancy and mental illness illustrated by the example above, an elaborate theoretical framework has been created and developed by theorists faithful to the CBT tradition. At heart they have remained true to the underlying principle that *real* mental disorders exist. This may very well be the case, though it does not automatically follow that all claimed disorders are real disorders. CBT like many other theoretical frameworks fails to tackle this issue (Not unlike many other health professionals, ontological and epistemological issues pertaining to 'mental disorders' are fudged by CBT practitioners in order to create seemingly convincing arguments). Indeed, most of the evidence supporting the use of CBT has been disorder-specific. In a peculiar way, the CBT framework produces a circular argument. CBT provides credibility for the notion of discrete separable mental disorders, which can be treated with CBT—which in turn provide CBT with its credibility.

The framework of CBT makes it clear that individuals have habitual ways of thinking. In its framework some are good and some are bad; or to use the lexicon of the discipline, negative and positive. How one arrives at ostensibly moral decisions regarding the goodness and badness of thoughts, even if one were to gain accurate access to them is unclear, and CBT does not seem to consider this exploration to be a worthwhile endeavour. Consequently, the vital question as to who decides what is good and bad is left unanswered. One can only but speculate that, not unlike most dominant discourses of society, such decisions are derived from the morality of the classes with influence in society. CBT thus insists that people subscribe to its framework because it is "scientific". In so doing, it keeps its clients subjected to the frame in which a bourgeois morality can be perpetuated. The individual suffers from a dual but simultaneous oppression. Firstly CBT imposes a structure of thought that he/she is not allowed to question; secondly CBT ascribes values to its content that cannot be challenged.

If health and illness are not as clearly defined as we would like, then popular opinion asserts that at least we can turn to science for clear unambiguous answers about how to treat mental illness. CBT is paraded as a treatment that is evidence-based. Can we rely on this evidence? The next few paragraphs briefly outline the critique of scientific endeavour that has been mounted over the last fifty years.

In the 1960s, Thomas Kuhn published a book entitled *The Structure of Scientific Revolutions*. He pointed out that in many fields there is a prevailing method of thinking which dominates, often for centuries. When a radically new idea, let us call it a "brain wave", comes along which requires the abandonment of old forms of thinking—an example might be the work of Kepler on the elliptical paths of the planets—then the new idea may struggle for some time. On the face of things, the brain wave may indeed not necessarily represent a clean break from the old ideas or it may seem counter-intuitive. Kuhn argued that eventually a new paradigm will replace old paradigms. By definition, the new paradigm will only give a very partial account of the field because scientific enquiry takes place on such an enormous and wide-ranging scale that most scientists spend their working lives exploring one small aspect of knowledge. What Kuhn fails to account for is the *logical* (as distinct from historical or political) reasons for the substitution of one paradigm for another. It is clear that the understanding of the nature of science itself changed dramatically between the end of the middle ages and the present day. Kuhn does not make clear *why* this should be so.

Where Kuhn and Popper differ, is in their reaction to accommodating (or otherwise) problematic facts, which often stand in the way of producing all-embracing potentially universally applicable theories. During the same era, Karl Popper published a book entitled *Conjectures and Refutations: The*

*Growth of Scientific Knowledge.* Popper's theories criticized science that is based on inductive thinking. He showed that such research is based upon the assumption that the basic premises involved are *not* in themselves derived from a set of assumptions which in turn should have been problematised. A kind of circular argument is then set up. The popular response to this conundrum is simply to assume that, "Never mind—of course we are asking the right questions" and, "of course we know that we can trust the answers". The remainder of this chapter will demonstrate that these assumptions are questionable on many counts.

Imre Lakatos criticised both Kuhn's and Popper's points of view. In a closely-argued posthumously-published book, *Proofs and Refutations*, Lakatos takes the reader through the logic involved in analysing some apparently straightforward mathematical proofs. If inductive logic is fallible, then can we fall back on deductive logic? Lakatos suggests not:

> In deductivist style, all propositions are true and all inferences valid. Mathematics is presented as an ever-increasing set of eternal, immutable truths. Counterexamples, refutations, criticism cannot possibly enter. An authoritarian air is secured for the subject by beginning with disguised monster-barring and proof-generated definitions and with the fully-fledged theorem, and by suppressing the primitive conjecture, the refutations and the criticism of the proof. Deductivist style hides the struggle, hides the adventure. (Lakatos, 1976, p. 142)

In the above quotation, for the term, "mathematics", we can of course substitute words such as "psychology" or "CBT".

Paul Feyerabend was both Lakatos' close friend and his chief theoretical critic. He dismissed all the theories of Kuhn, Popper and Lakatos. He claimed they were merely attempts to impose a rational belief system (however loose) and a methodology (however vague) in order to produce the illusion of some kind of logical progress on a series of random events. Controversially then, he argued that advances in science are largely the result of the take-up of ideas for often dubious reasons associated with pragmatism, financial gain, prevailing cultural fashions and pure accident. Feyerabend's writing suggests that "scientific progress" is often rewritten after the event in order to provide a smooth and coherent account to later generations. According to him, the history of science is littered with mistakes, errors, fraudulent research and discoveries that owe their existence to accident rather than coherent planning and pure scientifically rigorous thinking. Many of the arguments put forward by Lakatos and Feyeraband are clearly outlined in a book entitled *For and Against Method* edited by Matteo Motterlini and published posthumously after their deaths.

When people discuss the philosophical background to scientific research, they often prefer to adopt Kuhn's point of view since it allows the dominant research of a period to proceed without serious challenge. However, as this series of arguments shows, unquestioning adoption of one theory in preference to another should at least give us pause for thought and careful consideration.

The concerns discussed above merit few if any lines of comment in research papers of the kind where CBT is the subject of debate. The implication of the Kuhn/Popper/Lakatos/Feyerabend debate is that empirical science relies on an inductivist understanding of the relationship of truth to knowledge. Thus the propositions which underpin the questions to be examined "scientifically" are already assumed to be the "correct" questions. There is no room in this approach to research for inserting a fundamental hypothesis raised by researchers outside the field. One very troubling hypothesis might be, "All talking therapies including CBT are placebos". Where would this leave the evidence base for CBT and indeed other therapies?

Following the arguments set out above, it is possible that we may find in future years that CBT has been successful because its proponents were the most influential in obtaining funding rather than because CBT is inherently better than other forms of treatment. For those engaged in CBT research, there is of course no way of knowing whether or not such a statement is true or false. However, the reader may wish to bear the debate outlined above in mind.

## Statistical arguments

We shall now look at the evidenced-based approach to CBT. Research about both genes and the effects of medical treatments are apparently straightforwardly measurable. For those readers who are interested, we have included a more detailed critique to be found in the Appendix at the end of the book. Each type of research is carried out by people who have good clinical and scientific credentials. If these accounts constituted the whole truth, then scientific research would be on an ever upward curve; "cures" would be found for everything. In another sense, research would become a very strange animal. The role of the thinking human being constantly interacting with his or her environment would be absent. Human beings would merely exist, robot-like. Our genes and the effects they generate would be held to be responsible for everything. Once deficits or problems had been identified, it would then simply be a matter of carrying out the appropriate neuroscientific research and devising a gene replacement therapy which would correct any deviant behaviour. Deviant behaviour would be identified by applying the right psychological tools for measuring depression and the like.

A common way of thinking is often found in press reports which claim that certain conditions—depression and schizophrenia are common examples—are caused by our genetic make-up. The sufferer, their families and the environment and culture to which the research refers are therefore exempt from any influence. Nature apparently has triumphed over nurture. It is simply our bad (or very occasionally good) fortune to be born with a condition. There is another kind of evaluation that takes place here; the identification of genes and chromosomes with particular kinds of associated behaviour which can be statistically separated from other types of human behaviour.

There may be manifold problems relating to empirical research; nevertheless, recent years have produced an ever-increasing evidence base, which has been comprehensively reviewed by Roth and Fonagy in their book, *What Works for Whom? A Critical Review of Psychotherapy Research*. They are quick to point out that all research involves compromise and they devote a whole chapter to reviewing the many problems of methodology. One of the reasons for CBT's success has been the fact that it can be manualised. This means that there is a standard format and standard questions to be asked in a given order. CBT and other manualised therapies then have at least one stable component in the process of delivery. This promotes statistical research as discussed below. There is then at least the possibility of formulating a design which can produce results which satisfy some of the criteria of validity and reliability. CBT is sometimes delivered in the form of a computer programme thereby removing even more of the vagaries introduced by human unreliability.

We now turn to the evidence for CBT's effectiveness based on randomized control trials carried out by researchers on CBT. For reasons of space we have limited our survey to a few key papers which lay out the claims for CBT in the treatment of depression. Some readers may conclude that they simply do not have the background statistical knowledge to understand the complexity of the statistical arguments for and against CBT. However, for those who are interested in pursuing our conclusions in more detail, we have provided a brief summary of the papers discussed in the Appendix at the back of the book. Brief relevant references to these summaries appear in italics in the main body of the text to illustrate some of the points listed below.

The methodological problems relating to CBT are outlined very briefly. CBT's claims rest upon empirically tested scientific evidence. No set of statistics relating to human activity can ever be perfectly accurate. All designs carry some inherent flaws and often the aim of statistical design will be to minimise rather than eliminate possibilities of various kinds of error.

There are some key questions to bear in mind when considering any form of statistical evidence:

1. Are the variables measured in a study the "right" ones to pick?
2. Do they *actually* measure what they claim to measure?
3. Does the size of the sample of patients give us good grounds to believe that the statistics derived from the sample are reliable?
4. Has the sample been selected fairly, so that real comparisons are made between one kind of treatment and another?
5. Are the right statistical methods being used in research projects?
6. Are the results better than would be achieved by a placebo?
7. Can governments rely on the results of research and expect them to be replicated if CBT is the treatment of choice which thousands of people are trained to use with a very widely drawn population of sufferers?

All the CBT papers that we looked at contain problems with regard to one or more of the questions listed above. Turning from these very general statements, we list below some key terms used by statisticians to pin down questions like the ones above and then explain why they posed problems in the CBT studies we reviewed. Such terms include regression to the mean, small sample sizes, lack of clear definition of the factors being measured, inappropriately short follow-up times and often no clear evidence that CBT, or indeed the other control treatments, are better than placebo.

*Randomized control trial (RCT):* Statistical method often involves carrying out a randomized control trial where one or more research ideas are put forward and the researchers then design a trial to test these hypotheses. In the case of CBT, CBT has been compared with Interpersonal Therapy (IPT), placebo (see below) + clinical management, and drug + clinical management. There are a number of problems associated with RCTs that are clearly set out in a joint paper written by Jacqueline B. Persons and George Silberschatz.

This is a paper where two clinicians take opposing views on the issue of whether the results of RCTs are vital to practitioners. Persons, argues that RCTs are essential because the random assignment element of clinical trials provides "the gold standard of evidence about treatment efficacy." She claims, "RCT can answer the question, 'All the same, what treatment is best for disorder X?'" Unfortunately no paper can make clear assertions of this kind about CBT for reasons discussed elsewhere in this chapter.

For his part, Silberschatz does not directly address the very obvious questions relating to the applicability of statistical evaluation of psychotherapy. Rather, he asks a more fundamental question—whether RCTs *in themselves* are useful to the clinician. He describes them as "horse race" studies. In other words, which method of treatment will produce the fastest cure? He cites the work of Seligman who points out that RCTs omit too many of the crucial elements of therapy as it is practised in the clinic. For example, therapy often:

- has no fixed duration;
- continues until the patient improves or terminates treatment;
- in clinical practice (we assume of the non-manualised variety), psychotherapy is self-correcting i.e., if something

does not work then the psychotherapist will try a different approach;

• the patient actively seeks a psychotherapist of their own choosing (often an important determinant for success of the treatment);

• is aimed at improving patients' general level of functioning not just removing or alleviating symptoms.

Both the protagonists agree that "idiographic" as opposed to "nomothetic" research might offer common ground. Nomothetic research is based on what Kant described as a tendency to generalize, and is usually found in the natural sciences. It describes the effort to derive laws that explain objective phenomena. Idiographic research is based on what Kant termed "a tendency to specify", and is typically found in the humanities. It gives an account of the effort to understand the meaning of contingent, accidental, and often subjective phenomena. However, here we come full circle because it is extraordinarily difficult to generalise from idiographic research for all the usual basic reasons put forward in statistical research. Silberschatz succinctly summarises the problem, "Patients are not equal, therapists are not equal, and the therapeutic interactions between them are not equal, regardless of how meticulously manualized the treatments may be" (Silberschatz & Persons, 1998, p. 132).

*Control group:* A control group is a group that is set up where some individuals are offered an alternative to the form of treatment being tested. The control group is often offered a placebo.

*The placebo effect:* The placebo effect is a fascinating and complicated phenomenon. Placebos work on the principle of suggestion. The classical illustration consists in telling two groups of people that if they take an unmarked white tablet, their pain will be relieved. One group will receive a pain killer, the other will receive a placebo—a white tablet that looks the same but which contains no active ingredient whatsoever. It is often found that both groups will report relief from pain. If the researchers want to prove that the painkiller is effective, then they will have to prove that the patients who took the painkiller were freer of pain than the others, perhaps that the effect of the tablet lasted longer and so on. What looked to be a simple question of pain relief has become something altogether more complicated. Although an action is involved—the act of taking the tablet—words are implicated too. The words may simply be implicit. People expect to feel better when they take tablets. The suggestion has been implanted, probably from early childhood, that medicines and tablets relieve pain. This is an idea formulated in words.

An even simpler version of the experiment above would be to tell one group of sufferers nothing at all. The other group will be told that their prognosis is good; their pain will be relieved. You can guess what happens. This second version of the placebo effect now starts to bear a close resemblance to the workings of psychotherapies including CBT.

*Confidence Intervals:* The confidence interval is a measure of uncertainty and is usually reported as 95% CI. This essentially means that 95 times out of a 100 we can be sure that the measured values will be in the given range. In the Appendix you will find:

> *Paper 1—no significant differences in cases of mild depression.*
> *In very severe cases superior recovery rates for both interpersonal therapy and imipramine + clinical management.*
> *Paper 2—no statistically significant differences during treatment.*
> *Paper 6—no statistically significant differences between CBT, IPT or drug + clinical management.*

*Regression to the Mean:* This phenomenon was originally illustrated by one of the fathers of statistics, Francis Galton. A seven foot tall man is taller than average. His son may well also be taller than average but is very unlikely to be as tall as his father. Over time, the average height of a population will regress to the mean. In other words, the heights of the majority will cluster around the mean (i.e. average) height of the whole group. In CBT studies this phenomenon needs to be taken into account when looking at outcomes. Will a group of patients maintain the improvements they have made over time—or is the improvement "a one horse wonder" and they will gradually stray back to the mean of moderate depression measured in the whole group? The more a sample group differs from the mean in a whole population, the greater the effect. See Appendix:

> Paper 3—starts with a large number of clients but, by the time participants are excluded for sundry reasons there is a question arising whether the "maintenance of gains" is simply an example of regression to the mean.

*Validity:* This term has several meanings in statistics. The simplest for our purposes is that validity refers to the degree to which a study supports the intended conclusions to be drawn from its results. See Appendix:

> Paper 4—At no point in the paper do the researchers consider whether the results of following up patients offered either CBT or IPT are simply responding to both therapies as a placebo.

*Reliability:* Reliability is the consistency of a set of measurements used to describe a test. If a group of CBT researchers repeated exactly the same research design on a different group of patients, how closely would the results of the second experiment match those of the first? Reliability does not imply validity. A reliable measure is one which is consistent. It does not mean that it measures what it is supposed to be measuring!. See Appendix:

> Paper 5 attempts to address this question. The paper tries to assess whether the rate of improvement observed in patients tails off when the number of sessions is increased from 8 to 16. The evidence is equivocal. By this time in the literature, there is already an assumption that short-term time-limited therapies should be the ones of choice. An interesting question

> *to ponder is whether longer-lasting therapies might achieve longer-lasting results. Although these would be more expensive in the short-term, they might pay for themselves over the course of time if they resulted in lower relapse and recurrence rates.*

Most of the papers we discuss in the appendix relate to problems with regard to CBT. In order to be fair, we need to acknowledge the even greater problems in assessing the efficacy of rival forms of psychotherapy. For this reason we discuss a paper written by a proponent of a different form of therapy. Elspeth Guthrie acknowledges the success of CBT, stating that, "The dramatic development of cognitive-behavioural therapy (CBT) over the past 30 years, with associated high-quality research into the evaluation of its treatment effects, is to be welcomed and applauded." She admits that psychodynamic psychotherapy research has lagged behind in comparison to the well-researched and adequately supported claims of CBT.

Guthrie advocates a particular variety of psychodynamic therapy, psychodynamic interpersonal therapy (PIPT). The latter is an attempt to synthesise the main features of psychodynamic principles with "humanistic and interpersonal concepts". Here are the main components of the model with the present authors' reservations or qualifications in brackets:

1. *Exploratory rationale* understood as "identify[ing] interpersonal difficulties in the service user's life" (This approach privileges external factors over intrapsychic factors, i.e., what is going on in the patient's mind); in PIPT the external interactions with others especially problematic ones are understood as resulting from the unconscious.
2. *Shared Understandings* understood as "try[ing] to understand what the patient or service user is really experiencing or feeling" (How can this be known? Commonly people *say* they experience or feel something but often this is modified

later). This kind of therapy privileges the here-and-now over both the past and the future; in PIPT the mixed feelings would be part of the process of developing a shared understanding through the development of a language, use of metaphors etc.

3. *Staying with feelings* interpreted as focussing on the "here and now" (The majority of patients have very mixed feelings, particularly when their past history plays a major role in their present predicament).

4. *Focus on difficult feelings* (Sometimes a patient needs to start with the "easy" feelings about which they can talk. Only later can they address more "difficult" [and often for good reason "hidden"] feelings). This is acknowledged but it is felt that the process of developing a shared language in the therapist-patient dyad is the process through which such difficult feelings can be explored and eventually rendered more manageable for the individual.

5. *Gaining insight* understood as drawing parallels or pointing out patterns in different relationships and thus linking hypotheses. (This is a very worthwhile aim but it does assume that the patient is capable of making such connections and understanding hypotheses).

6. *Sequencing interventions* before moving to understanding interpersonal difficulties, the model emphasises the importance of staying with feelings. (The same reservation applies here as to the item, *Focus on difficult feelings*).

7. *Making changes* The therapist should actively acknowledge and encourage important changes that the patient makes in therapy. (This statement assumes that the therapist "knows" which ones are the important changes. Often patients, if asked, will select very different aspects of the therapy as useful when this is compared with the therapist's assessment).

By listing our reservations about PIPT, the present authors are attempting to demonstrate that all therapies present problems when attempts are made either to compare one therapy with another or to isolate the precise means by which any one therapy actually works. Thus it would of course also be possible to raise the same kinds of queries and questions about the practice of CBT. The paper is notable for its acknowledgement that CBT does not work for everyone. The same can be said of all forms of treatment for mental illness.

The second half of Guthrie's paper moves on to summarise three main studies which compare psychodynamic interpersonal therapy with CBT. These are

A. The Sheffield Psychotherapy Project (SPP-1; Shapiro & Firth, 1987);
B. The Second Sheffield Psychotherapy Project (SPP-2; Shapiro et al., 1994, 1995); and
C. The Collaborative Psychotherapy Project (CPP; Barkham et al., 1996).

Guthrie suggests that the findings of both A. and B. show no significant differences between psychodynamic interpersonal therapy and CBT. In study C. attempts were made to replicate the findings of A. and B. in the clinic by recruiting subjects from NHS clinics. Guthrie reports that, "It is not surprising that the results in CPP were not as impressive as in SPP-2, as most therapies tested in a research setting, with highly selected service users, do not appear to perform as well in a clinical environment." and "There was a greater trend for their symptoms to recur" (Guthrie 1999: 141). Thus this paper confirms some of the doubts cast on the model of randomized control trials raised by Silberschatz above.

## Diagnostic arguments

Whatever the professional background of practitioners, they will frequently be confronted by a stranger who presents for treatment. Unlike some common physical illnesses, diagnosis is often difficult. A few may have very obvious symptoms such as anorexia. However in most cases practitioners make a diagnosis that is necessarily approximate. There are several diagnostic tools available, some of the most well-known of which are The Diagnostic and Statistical Manual of Mental Disorders IV (DSM-IV) and the International Classification of Diseases (ICD-10). Whereas it is tempting to view diagnostic categories as unproblematic representations of categories of real illnesses and disorders this might not be an accurate view. The most blatantly obvious fact is that both the DSM and ICD have had a number of revisions, each with its own classification differing from the previous one. One is reminded of the Chinese Encyclopaedia referred to by Foucault in *The Order of Things*:

> animals are divided into: (a) belonging to the Emperor, (b) embalmed, (c) tame, (d) sucking pigs, (e) sirens, (f) fabulous, (g) stray dogs, (h) included in the present classification, (i) frenzied, (j) innumerable, (k) drawn with a very fine camelhair brush (l) et cetera, (m) having just broken the water pitcher, (n) that from a long way off look like flies. (Foucault, 2006, p. xvi)

At the end of the day these are all rough and ready methods of classification. Unfortunately they all have problems. The first problem is how to work out what the symptoms or "properties" of a particular illness are and whether or not a patient displays corresponding symptoms. In the case of a physical illness such as red spots, there are a variety of methods of determining whether someone is suffering from rubella or chicken pox. However, in the case of mental illness, as Rachel Cooper points out:

> Unfortunately, it is quite possible for us to miss the mark and choose variables that do not correspond to true

properties. Thus, almost certainly 'distance from my desk' or, more seriously, 'being a schizophrenogenic mother' are variables that fail to measure genuine properties. ... An analyst who wants to pick variables that measure genuine properties must rely on the current best scientific theories. As such, a theory is needed to guide the choice of variables ... (Cooper, 2004, p. 17)

Cooper continues:

Although the selection of variables that measure genuine properties requires some theory, might it be possible to use a theory that is not among those about which different mental health professionals disagree? Unfortunately not. In a cluster analysis of psychopathology, biologically orientated psychiatrists will want to include biological variables but may well consider variables linked to 'defence styles' to be suspicious. Psychiatrists adhering to different theoretical frameworks will disagree. ... If the DSM cannot be theory-free, what theory does it use? I suggest, as have many writers before me, that the DSM tacitly assumes that some biological account of mental illness will prove to be correct. ... Unfortunately, biological accounts of mental illness are by no means uncontroversial. As the DSM tacitly assumes some biological explanation for mental disorder, the DSM categories stand, or quite possibly fall, with such an account. (Cooper, 2004, p. 18)

The problems that occur with the DSM also occur with ICD-10. In each case, practitioners often have to make quick decisions. From initial diagnosis, many will proceed to use a variety of assessment tools. There are few guarantees, as the literature shows, that assessment and diagnosis will be correct. Examples of individuals who have received multiple and sometimes conflicting diagnoses are legion. One attempt to improve matters is to opt for ongoing assessment with "measurement tools" such as CORE, the Beck Depression Inventory (BDI) or the Hamilton Rating Scale for Depression (HRSD) since these measures purport to show a patient's state of mind at regular intervals in the treatment. Scores can be read off against a scale and the seriousness of the depression noted.

However, this is still the "red spot" problem—it is simply repeated. A reading on a scale does not tell us why someone feels depressed, nor whether the treatment has been the key factor which has changed a measurement. Three obvious factors may affect the accuracy of ongoing diagnosis. Changes may be due to chance. To return to the example of redundancy discussed above, if a person who has been unemployed succeeds in finding a job, they are likely to feel less depressed, regardless of any treatment they may have received. Finally, people have a propensity for filling in questionnaires according to factors which are not necessarily envisaged by those who draw up the questionnaire!

## Skills for health and National Occupational Standards

We continue this chapter about evidence by discussing some aspects of the consultation that at the time of writing was still taking place between The British Psychological Society and Skills for Health in creating National Occupational Standards for CBT. One of the many consequences of an evidence-based approach to mental health is that it encourages the notion that treatment can consist of a fixed process.

The draft guidelines suggest that presenting problems may include, 1. social phobia, 2. specific phobias, 3. generalised anxiety disorder, 4. depression, 5. obsessive-compulsive disorder, 6. panic disorder and 7. post-traumatic stress disorder. There is no indication in this statement regarding how are these to be diagnosed and distinguished from each other; nor whether there are problems for which CBT is contra-indicated and if so, why. Several performance criteria are listed including the following. The authors' comments are included in square brackets:

According to the guidelines you need to:

1. adopt a consistently open, collaborative style, characterised by constructive curiosity, that helps the individual: [How is this evaluated and how does it differ from other therapies—if at all?]
2. develop hypotheses regarding their current situation and to generate potential solutions for him/herself [How does the practitioner test the hypotheses he/she has made?]
3. develop a range of perspectives regarding his/her experience [What is meant by "a range of perspectives"?]
4. adapt your therapeutic style so that it accommodates the individual's individual strengths, cultural background, life stage and cognitive ability [If this were to involve a contradiction in terms with the modus operandi of CBT, what should be done by the practitioner?]
5. appraise the individual's own beliefs about the problem, what they believe can be changed and the likely implications of these beliefs on motivation for treatment and subsequent relapse prevention [How—through direct questioning or by deduction, or a combination of both?]
6. link the covert nature of problems with the overt presentation of symptoms/problems in a way that feels supportive, validating and respectful of the individual [How are "overt" and "covert" distinguished? For example a patient may be well aware that they are depressed but not wish to admit as much. Who is doing the "feeling" here—the patient or the therapist?]

Later on in the document, the CBT practitioner is invited to perform the following:

7. assess the relationship between thoughts, feelings and behaviour and identify maintenance cycles. [Again this

may be easier said than done. Since CBT only claims to work at best with 50% of patients, some of its failures may be as a result of faulty evaluation in this regard.]

8.  identify the interaction between a specified set of target behaviours, physical sensations, emotions and cognitions. [This statement makes the assumption that the interaction between behaviours, physical sensations, emotions and cognitions is the key factor that needs to be addressed. Beck et al. and his successors may allege this is true but other kinds of therapy which make use of different foundational assumptions are equally successful in randomized control trials.]

9.  translate the individual's complaints into a meaningful set of target problems and treatment goals [CBT assumes that cognitions can be equated with meaning. The treatment goals agreed with the patient may therefore not necessarily have the same meaning for patient as they have for the therapist.]

10. develop openly with the individual a cognitive behavioural formulation which links the individual's symptoms and problems, the beliefs underpinning these symptoms and problems, and the life events, which may have activated the beliefs. [The assumption here is that making someone's beliefs conscious will alleviate their problems. Freud discovered in the early 1900's that, whilst this technique worked initially, after a while it ceased to be effective. It is just as possible that quite simply any kind of interaction with any kind of therapist is a placebo.]

11. describe the likely origins of the individual's core beliefs [Why—to what end? This may of course be good practice but there is no indication here as to why the knowledge of the origins of a belief should be helpful in achieving a cure. Furthermore, in order to explore the origins of a belief, it is necessary to depart from the here and now of current emotional distress, contrary to the treatment principles of CBT.]

12. review and revise the formulation and the treatment plan as needed consistent with emerging clinical information. [Does a treatment plan as distinct from a more open-ended approach, for example waiting to see what the patient wishes to discuss next, have any valid statistical evidence to confirm the adoption of this approach in contradistinction to other approaches?]

13. derive a general plan for therapy which links directly to the hypotheses contained in the formulation [This statement assumes that the hypotheses adopted are correct. Might it not be better to test the hypotheses first?]

The document continues in the same vein with precise recommendations regarding knowledge and practice. The whole tenor of the document is towards prescribing in minute detail the practice of CBT. However the Skills for Health draft has been extensively criticised by the British Psychological Society on the grounds that many of its precepts are too vague. Thus the important distinctions between the practice of CBT with those who are mildly depressed and those who are, for example, suffering from bipolar disorder are omitted. Whilst this stance is to some extent obvious, it is also ironic. The assumption is made by the leaders of the psychological professions that solutions lie in ever more detailed accountability.

A serious criticism can be levelled at this approach by applying the well-rounded attack launched on the culture of accountability in the 2002 Reith Lectures given by Onora O'Neill. The opening sentence of these lectures is as follows, "Confucius told his disciple Tzu-kung that three things are needed for government: weapons, food and trust. ... Trust should be guarded to the end. Without trust we cannot stand." (O'Neill, 2002, p. 3) O'Neill argues that the never-ending demands of the audit culture have left our society impoverished and weakened. Using O'Neill's arguments, if we want to increase trust and thereby confidence in the practice of psychotherapy, "we need to avoid *deception* rather than *secrecy*" (O'Neill, 2002, p. 72). As the psychoanalyst Darian Leader has pointed out, the imposition of state regulation on the psychotherapy professions will not prevent charlatans and malpractice. Indeed, it is not only ineffective in this regard; at the same time the endless demand for transparency risks ruining the very delicate fabric of words that forms the material of all talking cures. Much of the time patients cannot bear to think about or talk about their deepest anxieties. The purpose of all therapies is to negotiate these problems not to browbeat patients with an insistence that they make their most difficult feelings and thought instantly available and "transparent" to the therapist.

*CHAPTER FOUR*

# The advantages of cognitive behavioural therapy

R eaders of this book will be aware by now that CBT has a number of serious problems. However, we would not be doing CBT justice if we did not draw attention to its very real benefits and advantages. As we pointed out in chapter one, Aaron Beck was a conventionally trained psychoanalyst who faced very serious issues. The treatment he had trained to deliver was not effective, at least in the short term. Psychoanalysis might work in the long run but, as Keynes famously remarked, "In the long run we are all dead". The treatment method that eventually became CBT offers the very real prospect of quick relief for a wide variety of painful emotional problems. It is a much more proactive treatment than many other therapies. The patient is expected to work at getting better. They participate and collaborate in their treatment. For many people this format in itself is stimulating, refreshing and empowering.

As a result, expectations of CBT's efficacy and success are raised. It may actually be the case that CBT is not intrinsically as successful as the popular press would have us believe. However, success breeds success, and this very fact is responsible at least in part for the spectacular growth of CBT-based treatments. Much of this phenomenon may be caused by the placebo effect engendered in all talking cures. How placebos work and how successful they are, will be the topic of a later book in this series. Although placebos are often discussed in rather dismissive terms, they are extremely effective in bringing about changes for the better in people's lives.

CBT is primarily a time-limited and short-term intervention although there are situations where it is recognised that this is not beneficial and alternative more long-term approaches have been conceptualised and applied with some success. However, short-term or time-limited treatments do not necessarily equate with poor outcomes. In these circumstances, CBT is very good at delivering results. People feel better. They go back to work. They no longer experience a troubling and disabling symptom such as agoraphobia, panic attacks or depression. Rival treatments may be just as effective but some of them take longer before patients feel the benefit.

The claim that CBT can provide quick relief is a very important factor in the decision of governments such as the one in the UK, to promote it as a treatment of choice. Large numbers of people can then, at least in theory, be treated for relatively small sums of money. Resources are and always will be limited and imposing this very real concept of finitude to therapy may prompt both therapist and patient to focus on present and practicable ways of relieving emotional suffering. CBT is sometimes accused of being simplistic and is seen as a threat to more nuanced and intellectually grounded talking cures. It can be caricatured as a therapy designed to be put in manuals and then administered in a mechanistic fashion to patients who are seen as passive and in need of direction. However, despite its relatively simple methods and short time span, there is no clear evidence that CBT achieves significantly worse results than its rivals.

A related factor here is that CBT is a relatively simple therapy to teach a wide range of practitioners. Whereas psychotherapists and psychoanalysts undergo a part-time training lasting at least (and usually much longer than) four years in the UK, CBT, at least in its simpler versions, can be taught in a matter of months. In the UK at least, the training methods for CBT fall into two groups. Firstly, there are fully qualified psychologists who have extensive academic grounding (doctoral level training); and secondly other professionals from a wide variety of backgrounds such as nursing or counselling, for whose training psychologists are usually responsible. Sometimes people receive additional training if they are going to work with people who have more chronic problems or those with specific mental illness. One of the reasons for the growth of CBT is that it has been successfully manualised and specified techniques can be used that seek to correct the cognitive errors seen in patients consistent with the underpinning theoretical model of CBT. This potentially means that practitioners can be taught specific cognitive techniques and the practice of CBT in relatively short periods of time. The assumption is made that longer periods of training lead to greater levels of expertise. However, the evidence of several studies shows that experience rather than the qualification of a practitioner is a better predictor of effectiveness (Roth & Fonagy, 2005).

A short while ago, one of the authors attended an introductory day for those interested in training as CBT practitioners. It started with balloons. Five volunteers from the audience each blew up a balloon and stood in a row with the knotted end of their balloons in their mouths. One of the trainers for the day paraded up and down threatening the balloons with a brooch pin. In the end the only balloon she burst was her own. The point of the exercise was to demonstrate the build-up of anxiety. The author wondered whether the anxiety of the participants would have been different if they had held the balloons between their knees leaving them free to talk to each other. None of the organisers had thought of this twist to the exercise although they sounded interested in this suggestion. The point is a simple one. If people can talk to each other, then they feel less anxious and better able to cope. Being able to speak makes a difference. There is nothing intrinsically wrong with actions and encouraging people to act. However, the group of those in society who suffer from mental illness is primarily made up of people who have problems with what they *think*. Actions, whether undertaken by oneself or other people, form only a part of what we think about. CBT has little if anything to say about the properties of language. Yet, like many other forms of therapy, it relies upon speech both as the medium of communication and as a largely undefined means of recording the feelings of the patient.

Although CBT practitioners may have a very different kind of training compared to that of their rivals, all therapists, whatever their professional and theoretical background, share many basic tasks. Anyone who offers a "talking cure" of any kind has to listen to the patient. The simple experience of another person paying careful attention to what you say can be a hugely rewarding experience. This basic procedure can dramatically change lives. As indicated in the previous chapters, it is difficult to separate the active ingredients in any form of therapy, but CBT, in its most common, face-to-face mode of delivery, certainly meets the criterion of offering the patient the experience of being listened to.

All therapies require that the therapist respond in some way to the patient's distress, setting a whole curative process in motion. The difference between any therapy and an ordinary conversation is that the focus of the discussion is on trying to help the patient; the patient of course is aware of this simple fact. Just as with other therapies, CBT is practised by many people from differing backgrounds and with different levels of experience. Although some aspects of CBT may be homogenous, there is still room for the warmth of a particular personality or a reassuring smile. The experience of any therapy is thus in some senses unique both to the patient and the practitioner.

CBT is a treatment that is seen to be straightforward. It has a method which tells the practitioner where to start, what kind of information to obtain from the patient and then proposes a series of interventions such as:

- challenging negative thinking and directing the patient to find positive alternatives;
- setting homework; and then
- checking that the patient is carrying out the tasks proposed.

Other therapies may pride themselves on being less coercive; however patients are often desperate to be told what to think about themselves and given practical tasks to change their lives. Taking the moral high ground and allowing the patient to make their own judgement about what is good and bad in their lives may be ethically much less problematic than telling people how to live their lives and what to do. However, many patients are too upset and unhappy to worry about the social engineering aspects of CBT. This factor may be to all intents and purposes irrelevant to them if the daily grind of their suffering can be relieved.

CBT does not seek to change society, but on the other hand, it does not prevent anyone from so doing. It is not inconceivable that as a result of successful treatment with CBT, some people may feel liberated from their symptoms and able to bring about societal changes. Although CBT can be seen as coercive in its methods it is also a collaborative project between the therapist and the client. Even though the power differential in the consulting room may not be completely abolished, it would appear that the CBT framework goes some way to redress the imbalance—agendas for each session have to be negotiated; tasks and homework have to be agreed.

The views of the early researchers who attempted to evaluate CBT in comparison with other therapies deserve careful consideration. Irene Elkin reminds us that the number of people who experience everything from ongoing mild depression to serious mental illness is in all probability a staggering 1 in 4 people in the United States. There is no reason to suppose that the figures are markedly different elsewhere (Elkin, 1989, p. 983). CBT may not in fact truly be the new therapy to be hailed as the saviour of mental health treatments. It may not live up to the great expectations that have been generated for it by governments and health services. Nevertheless, compared to other possible treatments such as other forms of therapy or drugs, it might be less harmful and at least offers the hope of relief. The sad truth may be that depression and unhappiness is often the normal human condition for which there is no cure, unless we are prepared to give up some of the benefits of being people rather than mindless robots. It is not the fault of CBT that so many find this message intolerable and seek relief from emotional pain.

Cognitive Behavioural Therapists unlike many other practitioners in the field have been ready to subject their interventions to scrutiny and scientific enquiry. CBT of course embeds itself within a particular scientific empiricist tradition, dominant in the West. Whatever the shortcomings of such a tradition are, these traditions are currently accepted in our society. CBT has embraced the challenge of providing a talking cure which fits with contemporary views of accountability and empirical evidence. In so doing it has met with considerable success. Its rivals have often fallen back on shadows of mystique, tradition and dogma reminiscent of Mervyn Peake's *Gormenghast* novels written in the 1940s. The criticism of CBT from other quarters, however valid it may be, is often complicated and weakened by the lack of the kind of evidence put forward for CBT that in our current world has become essential for the promotion of new treatments.

Thus CBT has challenged what was formerly a rather closed system of research in the psychotherapy field. It has brought a breath of not always welcome fresh air to a world where assumptions of the most sweeping kind were often made on the basis of the experiences of a handful of patients. As a result, it is not surprising that CBT is the therapy with the broadest base of scientific evidence supporting its methods. This fact has increasingly provided the impetus for practitioners of other modalities of therapies to seek new and often more imaginative ways of engaging in research. CBT practitioners have led the way in this respect. It would be unfair to inveigh against CBT as a treatment merely because it was the necessary catalyst to stimulate change in other therapies. It needs to be assessed fairly on its own merits.

The theoretical underpinnings of CBT in their most basic form have much of what researchers describe as "face validity". On first acquaintance it is a clearly comprehensible system of treatment easily understood by both practitioner and patient, who both think it will work. CBT embraces an important shift of emphasis from the traditional medical model of dispensing knowledge. Thus the therapist, rather than taking up a position of knowledge, embraces the position of a facilitator, questioning here, prodding there, guiding the patient and in doing so equipping her with a stance to challenge and question what may appear as self-evident truths. At the same time the therapist is offering the patient tools that have the potential to give her a sense of controlling her own destiny. Whereas a caricature of CBT might refer to it as "thought control", it is an explicitly *collaborative* endeavour. Patients can and do skip their homework from time to time! The crux of the matter is that if the patient does not like a particular option, she can choose to ignore it. It is, after all, a useful reminder that in the cult film, *The Matrix*, it is the people on the inside who are apparently leading contented lives and only those on the outside (with insight) who live lives of torment and agony. People do have choices and if they so wish they can choose to conform to societal demands or indeed challenge them. Thus in *The Matrix* one character opts to return to the dystopian matrix, in order to lead a contented life! The distinction between choice and indoctrination in the practice of CBT is often very subtle.

Notwithstanding the critique to which Cognitive Behavioural approaches have been subjected from social, psychological and philosophical view points, it remains true that human beings suffer immense misery despite often spectacular improvements in material standards of living. CBT provides a means of intervention that is demonstrably effective (within the current accepted norms of scientific research) that helps people—if not to get rid of their misery—then at least to avoid their entire life being blighted by it. CBT makes the modest and realistic claim that, if not everyone then at least some can be helped. This approach emphasises the pragmatism that has enabled CBT to become one of the most prominent and successful psychotherapeutic interventions of our time.

# APPENDIX

There are hundreds of research papers examining the claims of CBT and its competitors. For our purposes we will restrict our review to papers dealing with depression, one of the most common complaints for which CBT is routinely advised. Within this still large area we will look at a small sample of the most frequently cited research papers. Since research in the field is predicated on the belief that in general evidence can be built upon the findings of earlier papers, we have deliberately concentrated on what we believe to be the earlier foundational papers in the field. We have tried to select a reasonably representative range of the kinds of research on which evidence relating to CBT is based. The papers are listed in date order starting with the oldest.

1. "National Institute of Mental Health: Treatment of Depression Collaborative Research Program General Effectiveness of Treatments" in *Arch. Gen Psychiatry*—Vol. 46, November 1989. Elkin et al.

This is one of the key studies comparing the effectiveness of brief Cognitive Behavioural Therapy (CBT) and Interpersonal Therapy (IPT) in the treatment of outpatients with major depressive disorder. Each of the psychotherapies was compared with clinical management plus placebo, and clinical management plus the anti-depressant imipramine. The conclusions were largely tentative. There were no significant differences between all four treatments if patients were suffering from depression that was classified as less than "severe". In cases of very severe depression "superior recovery rates were found for both interpersonal therapy and impramine plus clinical management" (Elkin *et al.* 1989, p. 971).

Interestingly this paper has a postscript entitled "Editorial Note (Especially for the Media)" where it is rightly emphasized that there is widespread untreated depression which is costly in both human and economic terms. Thus there is pressure on all concerned with the treatment of depression to try to find effective methods of treatment. Aptly, it concludes, "This unsurprising complexity and the richness of options should be a boon for patients—not an occasion for ontological debate or a sporting event for the pop-science media" (Elkin *et al*, 1989, p. 983).

2. "The Course of Depressive Symptoms Over Follow-up" in *Arch. Gen Psychiatry*—Vol. 49, October 1992. Shea et al.

The authors of this paper looked at "the course of depressive symptoms during an 18-month naturalistic follow-up period for outpatients with Major Depressive Disorder treated in the National Institute of Mental Health Treatment of Depression Collaborative Research Program." They limited their research to patient who received one of the following four options, two kinds of short-term psychotherapy, CBT, and interpersonal therapy IPT, clinical management plus imipramine hydrochloride (an antidepressant), and clinical management plus a placebo in place of the imipramine. The study found no statistically significant differences during treatment and it is interesting that it chooses to regard 18 months, the longest passage of time after which the effects of the original treatment was assessed as "long term".

The paper then struggles with the complex questions of how to distinguish "recurrence" from "relapse". These terms are, in effect, only distinguishable in an arbitrary sense. This paper does not explore any of the following:

- Why there is an arbitrary cut off-point in the distinction of the terms—less than two months is evaluated as "recurrence" and more than two months as "relapse";
- Whether a new event which prompts a "recurrence" might actually also be represented as a "relapse";
- Whether someone who needs "further treatment for depression" is actually suffering from a recurrence.
- The possibility that a patient could experience *both* a recurrence and a relapse;
- Why there is such an emphasis on speed of treatment—arbitrarily, 3 consecutive weeks is taken as a minimum length of treatment-time required to bring about change. The paper is silent about whether longer term therapy might be more or less effective than the 16 weeks offered to all patients in the trial.
- Given that there is some evidence that depression often remits naturally after a period of 12 months to 2 years, this paper does not comment on why the follow-up period only lasts 18 months. More interesting (and possibly more reliable) evidence might have been collected if the follow-up period had extended to some time beyond 2 years.

The failure to discuss any of the above questions makes the findings of the paper highly questionable. As indicated above, there is no detailed examination of the key assumption relating to description of relapse/recurrence or the selection of the periods of time involved. However, turning to the statistics relating to recovery, there is no encouragement here for extending such a survey. Only 20% of patients entering treatment initially recovered and then remained well. The paper states that, "The major finding of this study is that 16 weeks of these specific forms of treatment is insufficient for most patients to achieve full recovery and lasting remission" (Shea et al. 1992, p. 782).

As in the previous paper discussed, this paper assumes that the placebo effect can be differentiated from the effects that are presumed to occur as a result of treatment.

3. "Effects of Treatment Duration and Severity of Depression on the Maintenance of Gains After Cognitive-Behavioural and Psychodynamic-Interpersonal Therapy" in *Journal of Consulting and Clinical Psychology* 1995, Vol. 63, No. 3, 378–387. Shapiro, D., Rees, A., Barkham, M., and Hardy, G.

This paper follows up 104 clients by mail 1 year after completing either 8 or 16 sessions of CBT or Psychodynamic-Interpersonal Therapy (PI). It is notable that the sample is small particularly when the factorial analysis consists in classifications according CBT or PI, 8 or 16 session and 3 different groupings depending upon initial assessment using the BDI scale of mild, moderate or severe. This yields 12 groups requiring 10 in each group. Immediately problems of small sampling size are thrown up, exacerbated by the restrictive entrance to the programme detailed under the heading "Client Selection". The original research commenced with 540 clients restricted to the category of "professional, managerial and other white-collar workers suffering from depression." This sample yielded 120 clients for the follow-up survey. The initial findings are presented in a 1994 paper by substantially the same group of authors.

One of the implications of this paper is that it has to be read in conjunction with the earlier paper since essentially it shows that only a minority of all clients in the survey (29%—18 patients in terms of raw statistics) were asymptomatic on all 3 occasions of testing. We need to know whether it would have been expected in the original survey whether patients would have recovered anyway. The "maintenance of gains" has to be viewed against the backdrop of the problem of regression to the mean. The correlations quoted in this paper may be statistically significant but if the follow-up period were to be longer (a suggestion put forward in the previous paper discussed) and if the group of clients is highly selected, then are these findings as interesting as is proposed? The reasons given by the therapists for relapse/recurrence are extremely varied, suggesting that hypotheses which cover all eventualities for relapse/recurrence are too vague. The terms "relapse" and "recurrence" are not distinguished in this paper. The paper concludes that CBT is superior to PI (if treatment is limited to 8 sessions) "fully one year after termination" (Shapiro et al. 1995, p. 384). Again, however, the researchers are cautious. They point out that, "Fewer than one third of clients remained symptom-free over a year ..." (Shapiro et al. 1995, p. 384). Even these figures are complicated by the fact that the client group may have been skewed since they were professional, managerial or white collar workers. Furthermore, some suffered from comorbid disorders (i.e. suffered from something else in addition to depression). Initially promising results in the case of the latter group were not sustained over three months or a year.

The study produces differences between the CBT and PI—principally that PI is less effective if it is restricted to 8 sessions. There is little to choose between them when 16 sessions are offered, and in the case of CBT, the researchers suggest it works better with booster sessions. Nowhere in this study is the notion entertained that in fact the driving factor of change in CBT and PI is simply a placebo effect as a result of some, any kind of interaction with a therapist. The follow-up does not include a control group of clients who are offered a placebo with or without drugs. This is a major defect in the light of evidence in the studies already cited.

4. "Acceleration of Changes in Session Impact During Contrasting Time-Limited Psychotherapies" in *Journal of Consulting and Clinical Psychology* 1996, Vol. 64, No. 3, 577–586 Reynolds, S., Stiles, W., Barkham, M., Shapiro, D., Hardy, G. and Rees, A.

This study attempts to evaluate the changes brought about by both CBT and PI. It follows up the suggestion that therapeutic change is accelerated in time-limited therapy. The researchers found that "the trend toward more positive sessions was more rapid ... in 8-session treatment than in 16-session treatments" (Reynolds et al. 1996: 577). One of the differences between the two forms of therapy is that, whereas CBT therapists "damp down" negative feelings in the therapy, PI therapists may accentuate them in the early stages of treatment. Later on however, patients benefit from both approaches. Whereas the first group go on a steep curve of improvement right from the beginning, the second group (after the initial stages of increased emotional disturbance) catch up with them by the time 16 sessions have been completed. However, the apparent precision generated by presenting the data in this way may be misleading. One of the models posited for symptom-change as a result of psychotherapy is the assimilation model. The assimilatory stages are listed on the y axis of the graph as 0 warded off, 1. unwanted thoughts, 2. vague awareness-emergence, 3. problem statement-clarification, 4. understanding-insight 5. application-working-through, 6. problem solution and 7. mastery. This model assumes that human beings are goal-focused, solution-driven animals who start at the beginning of a given problem (0 in this example) and then work through it logical step by logical step to the end (7 in this example). Findings from the education of children which focus on concepts such as "readiness to learn", "discovery" methods, deliberately varied methods of teaching reading and so on, point to the problem with this assumption. There are many ways in which children acquire the ability to read. Each child may be very similar but they are also different from each other! The resultant diagram where attention and feelings are both mapped against this scale produces a nice wavy pattern but nothing much more. Another problem with this presentation of the data is that terms such as "4 understanding-insight" and "5 application-working through" are not separated from each other clearly nor are they tightly defined. The analysis of the content of the sessions is therefore vague. The study also assumes that a report of a "smooth" session is a good thing in itself. We are a million miles away from humanistic ideas of therapy such as catharsis—the liberation through expression of difficult feelings. Objectively speaking, there is no reason for assuming that sessions with smooth feelings should *de facto* result in a "better" (essentially in this study "quicker") recovery from depression. There seems to be little real difference between the therapies examined in this study.

The paper closes with an interesting series of remarks. The authors agree with Eckert that "an explicit time constraint can accelerate a therapeutic change." This statement raises a number of potentially interesting conceptual issues. Thus:

> Under what conditions can therapy be delivered in fewer sessions without distorting the nature of the therapeutic process? Are there some clients for whom imposing time constraints would be contraindicated? To what extent can therapy be constrained without imposing unacceptable restrictions on therapists and their clients? Henry, Strupp, Butler, Schacht and Binder (1993) found that therapists who were trained to use manualized time-limited dynamic psychotherapy often reported that their spontaneity and intuition were curtailed and that, after training, these therapists exhibited less warmth and friendliness and more authoritarian attitudes toward their clients. (Reynolds et al. 1996, p. 586).

The paper ends on an inconclusive note recommending further research.

5. "Dose-Effect Relations in Time-Limited Psychotherapy for Depression" in *Journal of Consulting and Clinical Psychology* 1996, Vol. 64, No. 5. 1–9. Barkham, M., Rees, A., Stiles, W., Shapiro, D., Hardy, G. and Reynolds, S.

This paper has two aims. One is to assess whether there is a negative-acceleration effect to be detected in time limited therapy when the number of sessions is increased from 8 to 16. To put this more clearly: does the rate at which patients show improvement during their recovery from the symptoms of depression start to tail off after 8 sessions? The second aim of the paper attempts to establish whether acute and chronic symptoms of depression change at a different rate from those connected with interpersonal relations. This is a tightly-argued paper which finds that there is no clear evidence for a tailing-off of the success rate of treatment. The authors admit that their evidence is in any case limited since, unlike other more ambitious studies, it has not compared open-ended therapies and/or therapies of longer duration. Common sense would suggest that eventually the dramatic changes of the early days of therapy would be replaced by a decline later. However there is only equivocal evidence at best for decline in the rate of improvement between 8 and 16 weeks. A question not addressed by the paper is whether prolonging therapy might prevent recurrence or relapse, much in the same way that, in order to achieve optimum results, children with buck teeth who have orthodontic treatment need to wear a retaining brace for many months after the initial brace has done its work of straightening their teeth. The second issue addressed by the paper, suggests that patients' symptoms of depressed feelings change much more than their interpersonal experiences. An unexplored hypothesis was whether changing a patient's relationship to the people around them might either require different or longer-term treatment than either the Cognitive Behavioural or psychodynamic-interpersonal therapy offered to them.

By this time in the literature, there is already an assumption that short-term time-limited therapies should be the ones of choice. An interesting question to ponder is whether longer-lasting therapies might achieve longer-lasting results. Although these would be more expensive in the short-term, they might pay for themselves over the course of time if they resulted in lower relapse and recurrence rates. Anecdotally, there is some evidence of a reluctance to explore the extent to which those who have been offered CBT have already had previous courses of this treatment. Similarly, there is little evidence of a willingness amongst professionals in the field to carry out research where "long-term" improvements are measured over a period in excess of two years.

6. Ch. 4 "The NIMH Treatment of Depression Collaborative Research Program: Where We Began and Where We Are". Irene Elkin.

This is a chapter in the well respected *Handbook of Psychotherapy Research and Behavioural Change* (Bergin and Garfield, 1994, 114–139). Some indication of the basic assumptions of this organisation can be gleaned from a quote from one of its website pages aimed at Grades 6–8 students in the United States, "Students learned that mental illnesses were like other diseases, a physical problem in the body that could be treated by doctors" (attributed to a Field-test Teacher).

One of the stated aims of this chapter is "to accumulate more 'definitive' knowledge about the effectiveness of various forms of psychotherapy" (Elkin, 1989, p. 114). Elkins describes a large scale research project carried out by the NIMH Treatment of Depression Collaborative Research Program (TDRCP) comparing:

1. CBT Cognitive Behavioural Therapy;
2. IPT Interpersonal Therapy;
3. IMI-CM drug (Imipramine Hydrochloride) + clinical management; and
4. PLA-CM (placebo + CM).

The treatment was carried on a 250 people diagnosed as depressed using the BDI (Beck Depression Inventory). The aims of the survey include an attempt to discriminate between CBT and IPT in terms of effectiveness and an attempt to establish whether psychotherapies were more effective than other treatments. The paper admits, "Follow-up comparisons between pairs of treatment conditions revealed no differences between the two psychotherapies or between either of them and IMI-CM."

The chapter starts with setting out the background against which research has been carried out into CBT. The driving force behind funding research is the increasing need for accountability. A clinical trial is defined as "essentially, a well-controlled outcome study that uses a common research protocol at two or more participating sites" (Elkin, 1989, p. 14). The collaborative study was originally launched in 1977. CBT and IPT were chosen because each had demonstrated some effectiveness and each had been manualised. If there was a good understanding that the effectiveness of therapies was indeed based on the assumptions of the therapies and the structures of the therapies themselves, then this might not be too problematic. However, there is a possibility that the mere presence of the therapist, regardless of the questions posed and the exchange of dialogue, is actually the most important determinant of the therapy. Furthermore, both CBT and IPT implicitly assume that the words used in the manuals have a universal meaning. The relationship of words, language and meaning, has in fact been a hotly debated topic for the last hundred years. The privileging of "behaviour", assuming we do not need to define this word in CBT and IPT, might therefore be more problematic than it seems. This problem is tacitly admitted in the design of this study (and many others), since the researchers have to resort to a less "wordy" therapy, impramine-hydrochloride, an antidepressant in conjunction with clinical management (IMI-CM) as a control. The researchers in this and many other studies also tried to find a credible treatment which did not contain "the active ingredients" of CBT and IPT. Again they had great difficulty in identifying such a treatment and resorted to pill placebo plus clinical management (PLA-CM). There is no evidence in the chapter that clinical management does not in fact contain the "active ingredient" (whatever that is) of CBT and IPT. Thus comparisons are made between four types of treatment offered, CBT, IPT, IMI-CM and PLA-CM. The paper found no significant differences between CBT and IPT together with good results for the condition where patients were offered a placebo plus clinical management (PLA-CM). Only in the case of more severely depressed patients was it less effective. Interestingly for this category of patients, the option of imipramine plus clinical management (IPT) was the most effective. The general conclusion of the chapter is, "... [T]he general lack of significant differences ... between either of the psychotherapies and PLA-CM did not seem due to poor performance of the psychotherapies, but rather to quite good outcome for the patients in PLA-CM, at least in the less severely depressed subsample. ... [T]hese results must raise some questions about the specificity of the effects of the psychotherapies, particularly CBT." (Elkin, 1994, p. 130)

The chapter is studded with cautious references to the problematics of defining research in a field where language and the impact of the placebo is constantly undermining any attempt to elicit the precise dimensions—either of depression itself or of the cure on offer—of whatever kind. Elkins points out that PLA-CM is *not* a no-treatment condition and observes that it is effective in the hands of experienced clinicians. At the end of the chapter Elkin remarks almost wistfully, "Perhaps the field would be best served were we to stop using the term *'placebo'* and instead focus on the specific 'extraneous' or 'irrelevant' factors that we wish to control in order to isolate, as best we can, the influence of the variables in which we are most interested" (Elkin, 1989, p. 136). At least one commentator in the field of placebo research regards the proposition that all psychotherapies are in fact a form of placebo as self-evident (Moerman, 2002, p. 93–4).

To summarise, "The main reason for the general lack of significant findings seems to be due, not to lack of improvement in the psychotherapy groups, but rather to the very good performance of the PLA-CM condition. This is in contrast to the finding of fairly poor performance of waiting-list or delayed-treatment groups used as controls ..." Rather depressingly, the author also observes, "What is most striking in the follow-up findings is the relatively small percentage of patients who remain in treatment, fully recover and remain completely well throughout the 18 month follow-up period" (Elkin, 1989, p. 131).

# REFERENCES

Andrews, G. (2001). "Should depression be managed as a chronic disease?" in *BMJ*, Vol. 322: 419–21.

Barkham, M., Rees, A., Stiles, W.B., Shapiro, D., Hardy, G. and Reynolds, S. (1996). "Dose-Effect Relations in Time-Limited Psychotherapy for Depression" in *Journal of Consulting and Clinical Psychology*, Vol. 64, No. 5. 1–9.

Beck, A.T., Rush, A.J., Shaw, B.F. and Emery, G. (1979). *The Cognitive Therapy of Depression*, New York: Guildford Press.

Beck, A.T., Freeman, A. and Davis, D.D. et al. (2004). *The Cognitive Therapy of Personality Disorders*, New York: The Guildford Press.

Beck, A. www.beckinstituteblog.org (Consulted 06-07-09).

Beck, J. (1995). *Cognitive Therapy: The Basics and Beyond*, New York: The Guildford Press.

Clark, D.M. and Fairburn, C.G. (Eds.) (1997). *The Science and Practice of Cognitive Behaviour Therapy*, Oxford: Oxford University Press, 67–92.

Cooper, R. (2004). "What's Wrong with the DSM?" in *History of Psychiatry*, 15; 5 Downloaded from http://hpy.sagepub.com.

Davidson, K. (2000). *Cognitive Therapy for Personality Disorders*, Oxford: Butterworth-Heinemann.

Dennett, D. (1991). *Consciousness Explained*, London: Penguin.

Elkin, I. et al. (1989). "National Institute of Mental Health: Treatment of Depression; Collaborative Research Program General Effectiveness of Treatments" in *Arch. Gen. Psychiatry*—Vol. 46, November 1989.

Elkin, I. (1994). In *Handbook of Psychotherapy Research and Behaviour Change* 4th Edn. Bergin, A.E. & Garfield, S.L. (Eds.) (1994). New York: Wiley. 114–139.

Foucault, M. (2006 [1970]). *The Order of Things*, London: Routledge.

Guthrie, E. (1999). "Psychodynamic Interpersonal Therapy" in *Advances in Psychiatry Treatment*, Vol. 5. 135–145.

Hale, N. (1995). *The Rise and Crisis of Psychoanalysis in the United States: Freud and the Americans 1917–1985*, Oxford: OUP.

Lakatos, I. (1976). *Proofs and Refutations: The Logic of Mathematical Discovery*, Cambridge: CUP.

Lakatos, I., Feyerabend, P. and Motterlini M. (ed.), (1999). *For and Against Method*, Chicago: University of Chicago Press.

Layard, R. (2006). "The Depression Report: A New Deal for Depression and Anxiety Disorders", London: London School of Economics, Centre for Economic Performance.

Makari, G. (2008). *Revolution in Mind: The Creation of Psychoanalysis*, London: Duckworth.

O'Neill, O. (2002). *A Question of Trust: The BBC Reith Lectures*, Cambridge, CUP.

Persons, J.B. and Silberschatz, G. (1998). "Are Results of Randomized Controlled Trials Useful to Psychotherapists?" in *Journal of Consulting and Clinical Psychology*, Vol. 66, No. 1. 126–135.

Popper, K. (1963). *Conjectures and Refutations: The Growth of Scientific Knowledge*, London: Routledge.

Pretzer and Beck (1996). In *Major Theories of Personality Disorder* (Eds.) Clarkin, J.F. and Lenzweger, M.F. New York: Guilford Press.

Rachman, S. (1997). "The evolution of cognitive behaviour therapy" in Clark D.M. and Fairburn, C.G. (Eds.) *The Science and Practice of Cognitive Behaviour Therapy*, Oxford: Oxford University Press. 3–26.

Reynolds, S., Stiles, W., Barkham, M., Shapiro, D., Hardy, G. and Rees., A. (1996). "Acceleration of Changes in Session Impact During Contrasting Time-Limited Psychotherapies" in *Journal of Consulting and Clinical Psychology* 1996, Vol. 64, No. 3. 577–586.

Roth, A. and Fonagy, P. (2005). *What Works for Whom? A Critical Review of Psychotherapy Research,* 2nd Edn, New York: Guilford Press.

Shapiro, D., Rees, A., Barkham, M. and Hardy, G. (1995). "Effects of Treatment Duration and severity of Depression on the Maintenance of Gains After Cognitive-Behavioural and Psychodynamic-Interpersonal Therapy" in *Journal of Consulting and Clinical Psychology* 1995, Vol. 63, No. 3. 378–387.

Shea, M. et al. (1992). "The Course of Depressive Symptoms Over Follow-up" in *Arch. Gen Psychiatry*—Vol. 49, October 1992.

Teasdale, J.D. (1997). "The relationship between cognition and emotion: the mind-in-place in mood disorders" in Clark D.M. and Fairburn, C.G. (Eds.). *The Science and Practice of Cognitive Behaviour Therapy*, Oxford: Oxford University Press, pp. 69–93.

Ultrasis® www.ultrasis.com. Consulted 12.05.09.